Thematic Learning Centers

Illustrator:
Agi Palinay

Editor:
Mary Kaye Taggart

Editorial Project Manager:
Karen J. Goldfluss, M.S. Ed.

Editor in Chief:
Sharon Coan, M.S. Ed.

Art Director:
Elayne Roberts

Associate Designer:
Denise Bauer

Cover Artist:
Sue Fullam

Product Manager:
Phil Garcia

Imaging:
David Bennett
Ralph Olmedo, Jr.

Publishers:
Rachelle Cracchiolo, M.S. Ed.
Mary Dupuy Smith, M.S. Ed.

Author:

Katherine Ruggieri-Vande Putte, M. Ed.

Teacher Created Materials, Inc.
P.O. Box 1040
untington Beach, CA 92647
ISBN-1-57690-033-9

©1996 Teacher Created Materials, Inc.   Made in U.S.A.

CL
E2 371.36

Table of Contents

Table of Contents (cont.)

Introduction and Overview

Thematic Learning Centers is a broad-based thematic curriculum for primary students. The concept of connections is explored through the topics *People*, *Environment*, and *Communities*. The objectives of this book follow:

- to create a broad-based understanding of connections through specific topics
- to provide a framework for exploring personal and communal connections
- to increase awareness of interrelationships among people, environments, and communities—both individually and communally
- to provide an opportunity for topic-specific creation and exploration
- to introduce and provide practice for information gathering and reporting skills

The following is a brief summary of each topic. Each topic presented is further defined by a statement identified as the *focus topic*.

People

Focus Topic: People Are Unique in Many Ways

This section introduces students to basic human understandings and the uniqueness of the individual. As students begin working in the learning centers, these high interest activities are easily completed and provide students with successful first experiences.

Environment

Focus Topic: Environments Require Care

This section provides a wider perspective by introducing the concept of combining efforts to achieve a desired effect. The learning center activities deal with the concepts of reusing, recycling, protecting, conserving, and appreciating the complexities of nature.

Communities

Focus Topic: Communities Need Cooperation

This focus topic explores communities and the cooperative element needed as communities are created and maintained. The learning center activities examine the basic functions of a community, and they offer the students opportunities to be members of a community.

Each topic is presented through five classroom learning centers. *Thematic Learning Centers* begins at an introductory level with the topic *People*. One activity is presented in each learning center for this topic. However, for the other two topics, *Environment* and *Communities*, each learning center has more than one activity. The teacher may choose to present just one activity for each learning center or may include more than one.

Using the Book

Each of the three section topics is presented through center planning sheets, center descriptions, support materials, daily lesson plans, Bloom's Taxonomy activity cards, problem solving activity sheets, and a connection activity sheet.

Center Overview Pages and Center Planner: These pages are designed to give the teacher a complete picture of the learning center activities offered in each section. This allows the teacher to determine the difficulty and direction of the activities. The planning grid can be copied and used to record information that will be helpful in preparation, scheduling, and assessment. The teacher can use this page when deciding which activity will go in which center. The space after the center number can be used to write the name of the center in which the activity will be done.

Center Descriptions: Each center description includes the objectives, materials list, activity description, teacher tips, extension ideas, and a statement for the student direction card. This information is designed to guide the teacher in preparing materials, introducing the center activity, and monitoring student work. The center activities (as explained in the center descriptions) are designed for two purposes: 1. to provide the teacher with introductory activities to be used with the whole class and, 2. to describe activities to be done by individual students in the learning centers. Support materials are provided for the centers when necessary. These support materials are copy ready. Also, copy ready student direction cards can be found at the back of the book.

Daily Lesson Plans: The daily lesson plans are designed to supplement each topic. The lessons can be done at any time during the topic presentation. Daily lesson plans are designed to be presented as whole-class activities. Each daily lesson plan contains its own objectives to help the teacher relate it to the focus topic.

Bloom's Taxonomy Activities: These activities provide an opportunity to introduce your students to Benjamin Bloom and his levels of thinking. Bloom's Taxonomy describes six levels of thinking, beginning with *Knowledge* and concluding with *Evaluation*. The thinking levels may be described simplistically as shown below:

Knowledge—what is learned

Comprehension—what is understood

Application—the use of acquired and understood information

Analysis—examination of information

Synthesis—reaction based on learning

Evaluation—the judging and reviewing of information

Using the Book *(cont.)*

Bloom's Taxonomy Activities *(cont.)*: Activities covering the first three thinking levels are provided in the first two focus topics. The last three thinking skills are presented in the third focus topic. Each taxonomy activity is written in a shape representing the focus topic. The taxonomy shapes are designed to be copied onto construction paper (or index stock), cut out, and laminated. The activities can then be posted in the centers for your students to use, or they may be used as seat work by individual students.

Problem Solving Activities: Problem solving activities are presented in each focus topic. These pages provide an opportunity for the students to take their knowledge of the focus topic and apply it to real life situations. The activities can be done as a class, in small groups, or individually.

Connection Activities: These activities are designed to be culminating activities for the focus topics. There are many ways the teacher can utilize them. They can be used to assess student understanding of the focus topics, explore and debate issues, or increase flexible thinking in relation to the topics. Vocabulary for the activities can be teacher-generated, or the class can decide the vocabulary. These pages are designed to encourage students to explore and expand their concepts of connections. Students can work with one focus topic or encompass all three of the focus topics presented in the book.

Student Directions Cards (pages 135–144): The final pages of this book are filled with the Student Direction Cards. There is one card for every center activity described in the preceding three sections. Reproduce and cut out the cards. Glue them to large index cards or other heavy paper. You may wish to laminate the cards for durability. Place them in the appropriate centers. The cards will explain each center assignment to your students.

Scheduling the Units: There are several options for scheduling the units into your school year. Be sure to consider other curriculum commitments, district programs, and testing schedules as you plan. The book is divided into three topics, each designed to take from five to eight weeks to present.

The following are suggested time lines for completing the three sections of this book.

Fall Start	Winter Start
October, November—People	*December, January*—People
December, January—Environment	*February, March*—Environment
February, March—Communities	*April, May*—Communities

Learning Centers

Preparing the Learning Centers

Learning centers can be set up in a variety of ways. Be sure the set-up option you choose is compatible with your classroom space and your teaching style. If you have room, you may want your learning centers to be permanent areas of the room. When making permanent centers, label each one with a center name. Names can be animals, numbers, famous people, or a combination of these. If you choose permanent learning centers, be sure that each center has storage room (baskets, shelves, tubs) and an information area for posting student direction cards and sample work.

Centers can also be created by using large storage tubs with lids. Tubs can contain all of the necessary materials for the center and can be brought out for students to use at their desks or worktables. Student direction cards and sample work can be taped to the insides of the tub lids and be displayed when the centers are being used.

Using the Learning Centers

In the learning centers students will work in both individual and cooperative modes. As students begin working in learning centers, some general rules and expectations should be established. Discussion topics should include the following:

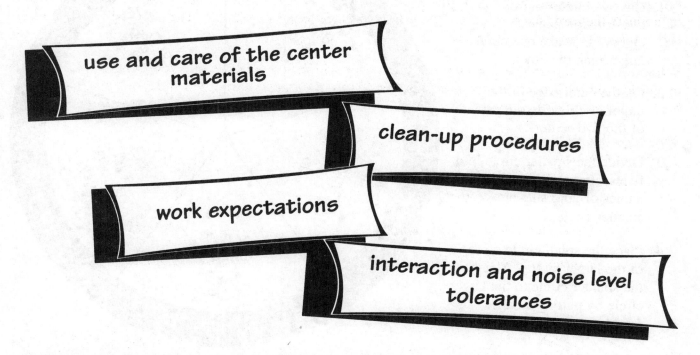

Do not expect your students to automatically be comfortable and self-motivated in the learning centers if this is their first experience using them. As they become more comfortable working in centers, their creativity and self-motivation will increase.

Scheduling: It is best to schedule several short time slots (30–45 minutes) during the week for learning center work. You may want this time to be directly connected to a whole-class directed work time so that your students can begin working in centers as they finish their classwork.

Using the Learning Centers (cont.)

Student Accountability: Student accountability can be handled in different ways. You should have a system in place that (1) ensures each student an opportunity to attend each center and (2) monitors student progress.

Center Cards: Small cards (index cards) can be used to record each student's progression through the centers. Each card should have the name of all of the centers and the student's name. As the student attends the center, the card can be marked with a sticker, teacher's initials, or a hole punch. The student will attend each center on the card before beginning the cycle again. A reward (sticker, treasure, applause) can be given each time the student completes all of the centers on one card. The student then receives a new card and begins the center rotation again. A progress sheet can be created by recording the date each student finishes each center card.

Center Wheel: A center wheel can be used to determine which group of students will attend which center. This works well if you want students to work with the same group of students as they go to each different center. To make a center wheel follow the steps below.

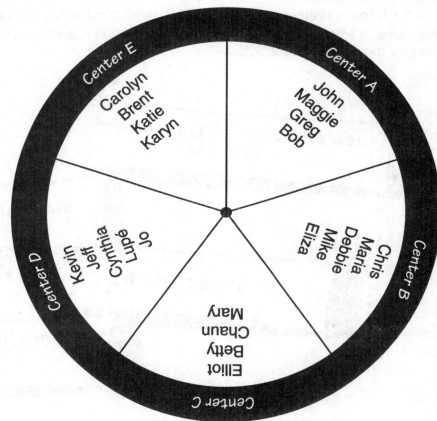

1. Cut two circles out of construction paper or tagboard. Make one circle larger than the other.

2. On the outer edge of the larger circle write the names of the five centers.

3. Divide the smaller circle into five sections. Write the names of your students on the smaller circle.

4. Place the small circle on top of the larger circle. Attach the smaller circle to the larger circle by putting a paper fastener through the middle.

Student Assessment: Student work should be assessed in a nonthreatening way. Have a box (or basket) where students can place finished center work. At the end of each day, take time to share the work in the box with the class. Make positive comments about each piece of work along with constructive suggestions (if necessary). Give the owner an opportunity to comment on his or her work if he or she wishes to. This sharing time will give you lots of information and will also be your best motivational tool once the centers are in use.

Overview of People Centers

Focus Topic: People Are Unique in Many Ways

Objectives

Students will . . .

  . . . understand the term "unique" as it relates to people.

  . . . recognize uniqueness in themselves.

  . . . recognize uniqueness in others.

  . . . explore personal feelings, characteristics, and ideas.

  . . . explore other people's feelings, characteristics, and ideas.

  . . . explore family relationships and ancestry.

Center Activities

On the blank lines write the names of the centers in which you plan to locate each activity.

Center #1 _____

My Unique Family

Using construction paper circles, students will create their family members, portraying the uniqueness of each member.

Center #2 _____

Me Book

Students will use the provided activity sheets to create Me Books, exploring information about and related to themselves.

Center #3 _____

Me Puzzle

Using drawing paper, students will draw pictures of themselves and create puzzles.

Center #4 _____

This Is Me

Students will find pictures in magazines that describe their personalities, likes, and/or hobbies and glue them onto body outlines, creating personal collages.

Center #5 _____

My Family Tree

Students will paint leaves with finger paints, representing members of their family on a construction paper tree.

Use this chart to plan your centers for this unit. On the blank lines write the names of the centers in which you plan to locate each activity.

People Center Planner

People Are Unique in Many Ways

1. _____	2. _____	3. _____	4. _____	5. _____
My Unique Family: Use construction paper circles to create each family member.	**Me Book:** Use provided worksheets to create a Me Book.	**Me Puzzle:** Draw a picture of self and create a puzzle.	**This Is Me:** Glue pictures representing likes, hobbies, etc., onto an outline to make a personal collage.	**My Family Tree:** With finger paints, paint a leaf on the tree for each family member.

Materials

Plans

Notes

Center #1

My Unique Family

Objectives:

Students will . . .

. . . explore the uniqueness of their family members.

. . . describe characteristics determining uniqueness.

. . . appreciate family members as being unique.

. . . portray family members' characteristics.

Materials:

❋ construction paper circles (various skin tones) copied from page 12

❋ art supplies, including paper scraps, markers, crayons, yarn, paint

Activity:

Have your students use construction paper circles to create the faces of their family members. Markers, paint, yarn, thread, material scraps, and paper scraps can be used to create family members. Encourage your students to recognize and display differences among family members. Differences can include physical traits and likes and dislikes, as well as personality traits. Traits can be written on the backs of the circles or depicted through the creation of the faces.

Teacher Tips:

When photocopying the circles be sure to use skin-toned construction paper if available. If skin tones are not available, be sure to provide skin-tone crayons or markers. When choosing yarn try to find hair-colored yarn—yellow (blond), orange and red (redheads), brown, and black. It may be helpful to cut the yarn into six-inch lengths so that the students can work with it more easily. White glue is best for this activity. Beans, buttons, felt, lace, paper scraps, and material scraps can be used for adding the details.

Extensions:

Have the students create family albums by gluing their family portraits onto construction paper pages. Family albums can be supplemented by adding actual photographs of family members.

Student Directions Card:

Using the materials provided, create each member of your family. On the back of the portraits write things about each person which make him or her unique.

My Unique Family *(cont.)*
Cut out the circle. Color and decorate to make a family member.

Center #2

Me Book

Objectives:

Students will . . .

> . . . explore information related to the self.

> . . . share information related to the self.

> . . . describe themselves through drawings.

> . . . learn more about themselves through measurement.

> . . . recognize themselves as important.

Materials:

- ❋ construction paper covers for each Me Book
- ❋ Me Book pages (see pages 14–18)
- ❋ paper clips, erasers, measuring tapes, and playing cards for measuring (see page 17)
- ❋ pencils
- ❋ crayons

Activity:

Introduce each page from the Me Book to the students, explaining how each page is to be completed. Allow your students to ask questions and express concerns. Encourage the students to incorporate details into their drawings. Require correct and careful spelling on their written work.

Teacher Tips:

Make a sample Me Book about yourself to show your students. Discuss each page as you share your book with the class. Students will love to hear all about you, and you will have an opportunity to show your work expectations, (e.g., color and detail in the drawings, correct and neat spelling).

Extensions:

Before sending them home, display Me Books in a class binder for several days so that the students can read about their classmates. Pages that reinforce current curriculum can be added to the Me Books (such as a map of the student's neighborhood, an hourly chart of daily activities, a written interview with someone in the student's family).

Student Directions Card:

Using the pages provided, create a Me Book. Use color and detail in your work. Be sure to write and spell carefully.

This Book Is About . . .

_____

A Very Important Person!

Draw yourself here.

Center #2

My Favorite Things

Draw or list your favorite things.

Colors

Foods

Animals

Books

Hobbies

Places

Center #2

Facts About My School

Fill in the blanks.

My school is called _____.

I am in the _____ grade.

My teacher's name is _____.

I am in room _____.

I _____ to school.

School starts at _____.

The rules we follow are these:

_____

_____

_____

_____

_____

_____

Center #2

All About Me

Fill in the blanks.

My name is _____.

1. I am _____ hands tall.

2. The distance around my head is _____ small paper clips.

3. My hand is _____ pencils long.

4. My arm is _____ hands long.

5. The distance around my elbow is _____ inches.

6. The distance around my foot is _____ small paper clips.

7. The distance around my knee is _____ inches.

8. My wrist is _____ erasers from my elbow.

9. My little toe is _____ inches long.

10. My thumb is _____ erasers from my pinkie.

11. My leg is _____ playing cards long.

12. My hair is _____ inches long.

(**Teacher's Note:** For metric measuring, replace the inches with centimeters before copying.)

Center #2

If I Were in Charge of the World, I Would . . .

If you were in charge of the world, what would you do? Draw or write your ideas in the globe below.

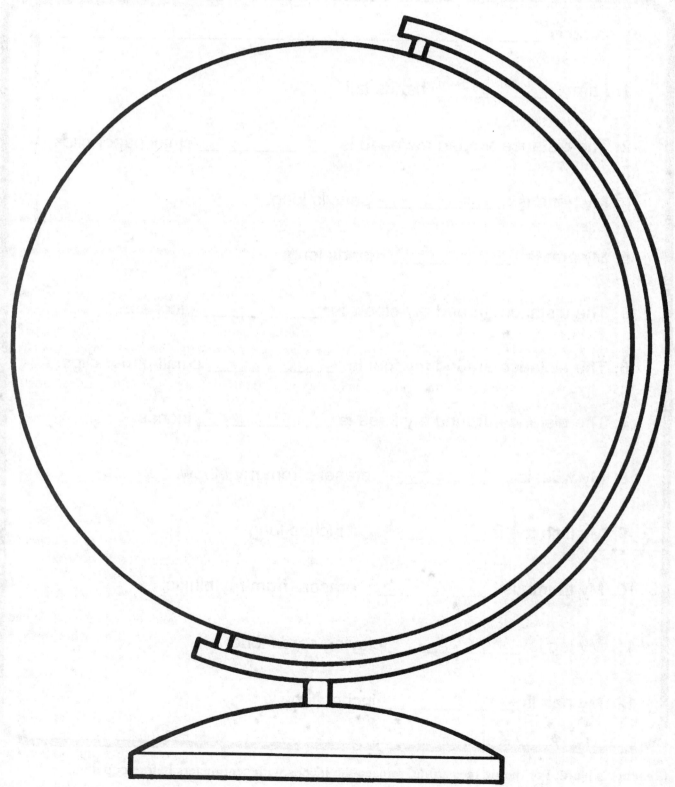

Center #3

Me Puzzle

Objectives:

Students will . . .

> . . . describe themselves through drawings.
> . . . create puzzles.

Materials:

* drawing and construction paper
* large envelopes
* markers and/or crayons
* full-length mirror (optional)

Activity:

Have each student draw a picture of him/herself on large drawing paper. Encourage your students to pay attention to proportional details. You may want to have access to a full-length mirror for this activity. After the students complete their drawings, have them mount their art on construction paper. (Students will need to be sure the entire back of the drawing is covered with glue. Glue sticks work the best.) Then have the students draw light cutting lines on the back of the construction paper to create eight equal pieces. (The shapes of the pieces should vary.) Students will then cut on the lines, creating puzzles. Store the pieces in large envelopes labeled with the students' names. Students can personalize their envelopes with designs and drawings. Leave the finished puzzle envelopes in the center so that other students can try putting them together.

Teacher Tip:

Be sure to demonstrate the process so that the students will understand when and how to cut their puzzles.

Extensions:

Envelopes can be labeled by student-created codes instead of names. This will allow other students to guess who is in the puzzle pictures. A chart can be made from a class list to record the students' guesses. Ask the students to record the codes which they think belong to each student next to the students' names on the list. Identities can be revealed once everyone has had a chance to guess.

Puzzles can be saved in their envelopes and used for a class puzzle party. At the puzzle party give each student a puzzle to put together. When a student finishes assembling a puzzle, give him or her the opportunity to guess who created it. Prizes can be given for correct guesses and for good tries.
(If prizes are used, be sure everyone gets one.)

Student Directions Card:

Use the drawing paper to draw a picture of yourself, including as much detail as possible. Then glue your drawing to a piece of construction paper. Next, draw light cutting lines on the back of the construction paper. Make eight sections about the same size but different shapes. Now, cut on the lines to create your puzzle. Store your puzzle in a large envelope.

Center #4

This Is Me

Objectives:

Students will . . .

    . . . describe themselves through collages.

    . . . share aspects of themselves.

Materials:

* outline of person to enlarge (page 21)
* tagboard or cardboard
* large paper
* magazines
* scissors
* glue

Activity:

Prepare a tagboard (or cardboard) pattern of a person by first enlarging the outline on page 21. Then draw it onto the board and cut it out with an art knife. Have your students trace the pattern onto large pieces of paper and then cut them out. The people cutouts should be labeled on the back with each student's name. Your students may then find pictures in magazines of things which describe something about themselves. Encourage your students to cut pictures out carefully, removing any unnecessary writing. Pictures can show likes, hobbies, personality traits, etc. Next, ask your students to create collages by gluing their pictures onto their people cutouts. Be sure to display completed work.

Teacher Tips:

Create a collage of yourself to show your students. Your collage can be laminated to increase its life span. Be sure your tagboard outline is a reasonable size. Too large an area to cover with pictures can discourage students. Too small an area can limit their creativity.

Extensions:

Finished collages make great decorations for classrooms, hallways, and school libraries. They are a big hit at Open House or Parent Nights.

Student Directions Card:

Trace the person pattern onto a large piece of paper. Write your name on the back of your traced person. Find pictures in magazines which show things about yourself—likes, hobbies, personality traits, favorite colors, food, movies, etc. Cut out the magazine pictures and glue them onto your paper, creating a collage.

Center #4

Person Outline

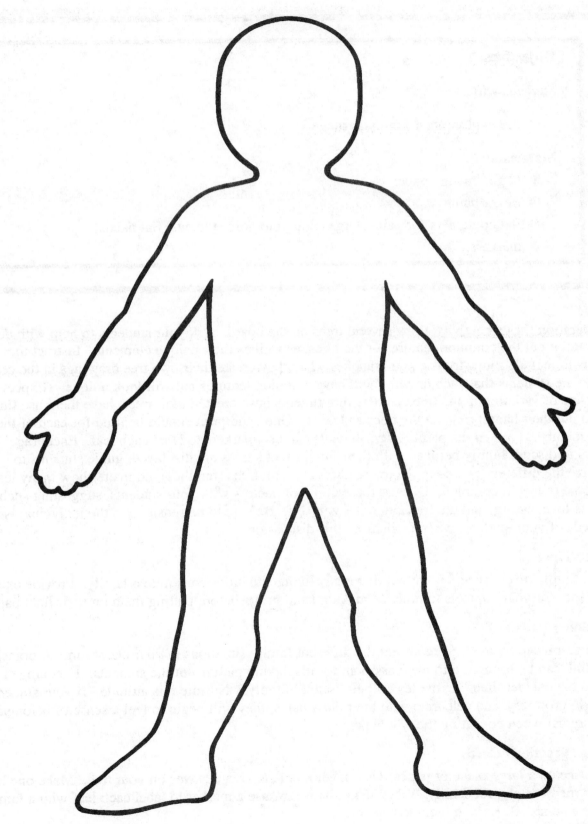

Center #5

My Family Tree

Objectives:

Students will . . .

    . . . explore their family heritage.

Materials:
- ❋ large drawing paper
- ❋ finger paint
- ❋ flat containers for paint (large enough to hold students' flat hands)
- ❋ markers

Activity:

In preparation for this activity, draw several trees on the board. Ask your students to help with design ideas. Point out the common features of the trees, as well as their unique elements. Instruct the students to include roots, trunks, and branches when they create their own tree drawings in the center. Remind the students that each drawing will have common features but will look unique. (Expect and accept lots of variation in the trees.) After the students have created their trees, have them use finger paint to put their hand prints on the trees as leaves. One hand print should be used for each of their family members. When the paint is dry, students can use markers to label each leaf. Encourage students to discuss family heritage with their families. As trees are displayed, guide students to recognize the differences among the trees. Stress that all trees (families), no matter how many leaves, have some things in common. Discuss these common factors with your students, suggesting such things as love, caring, and the freedom to be yourself. Be sure to be sensitive to the individual issues and needs of your students when facilitating this discussion.

Teacher Tips:

Discuss family diversity and point out that many living situations constitute a family. Provide extra scrap paper for your students to practice making hand prints before putting them on their final paper.

Extensions:

A class graph can be made to represent the different family situations in your classroom. A branch or small limb can be brought into the classroom for displaying pictures of the students. Encourage the students to consider their classmates as their "school family." Nurture this attitude. If your students can learn, grow, cry, and celebrate with their classmates, they will begin to feel a sense of belonging that is crucial when educating the whole person.

Student Directions Card:

Draw a tree on a large piece of paper. Use finger paints to create leaves on your tree. Make one leaf for each member of your family. When the paint is dry, use a marker to label each leaf with a family member's name. Be sure to include yourself.

Daily Lesson Plan #1

People Parts

Objectives:

Students will . . .

. . . explore the idea of people parts.

. . . identify positive and negative parts.

. . . identify their own parts.

. . . discuss feelings related to parts.

. . . record parts, using a people parts picture.

Materials:

❖ six construction paper squares 3" x 3" (7.6 cm x 7.6 cm) per student

❖ paper plates (one per student)

Activities:

1. Discuss the idea that people are made of many parts. Include your own parts in the discussion as an example. Use positive traits and characteristics, as well as less positive ones. Include skills, likes, dislikes, personality traits, and talents.

2. Describe a fictitious person to the students, including positive and negative features. Ask your students to identify the parts of the person described.

3. Have your students think about their own parts. Provide a safe environment for students to share positive and negative parts of themselves if they choose.

4. Facilitate a discussion on the feelings surrounding different people parts, positive and negative. Help your students to consider the advantages and disadvantages surrounding different people parts.

5. Have each student make a people parts picture. First, ask them to cut out six "crazy" shapes from the pieces of 3" x 3" (7.6 cm x 7.6 cm) paper. Then, have them write one of their parts on each of the six papers. Next, tell each student to draw his or her face on paper plates. The people parts can then be glued around the top edge of the paper plate, creating a unique person picture.

Teacher Tips:

Be sure to have ample time available when beginning the discussion. As students begin sharing, be flexible and follow their lead in the discussion, as this may be a time when students will feel safe revealing fears or doubts. Stress that everyone has both positive and negative parts.

Extension:

Have students write letters to themselves describing their parts. Each letter should begin "Dear Self, I see you are made up of many parts." Students can then go on to describe the many parts they see in themselves.

Daily Lesson Plan #2

I Am Unique

Objectives:

Students will . . .

. . . define the term unique.

. . . share something unique about themselves.

. . . observe connections between unique items.

. . . examine the relationship between unique and similar.

Materials:

❖ items from home

Activities:

1. Discuss with your students the term unique and develop a thorough and concise definition.

2. Ask your students to bring to school an object from home that is important to them or that describes a personality trait.

3. Allow your students to sit in a large circle and take turns sharing their items from home.

4. Encourage your students to notice similarities and differences among the items brought from home.

5. Give your students the opportunity to verbalize the connections that they see among the items brought from home.

6. Help your students to understand that things can be unique and also have connections.

Teacher Tips:

Be sure that you have created a safe and caring atmosphere as you begin this activity. Remind the students that the items being shared may be personal and have great significance to the people sharing them. Also remind them that teasing and criticizing are not allowed.

Extensions:

Have students pair up with partners whose shared items have something in common. Have the partners make a list of their shared and unique traits. Partners can share their list with the class.

Daily Lesson Plan #3

Which Is Which?

Objectives:

Students will . . .

> . . . define the term unique.
> . . . observe unique characteristics.
> . . . recognize unique characteristics.

Materials:

❖ unshelled peanuts (one per student plus extras)

Activities:

1. Pass out an unshelled peanut to each student.

2. Ask the students to examine their peanuts and note any unique characteristics. Be sure that the students do not mark on the peanuts in any way. Tell the students that they will have to recognize and claim their peanuts from a group of peanuts.

3. After the students have studied their peanuts carefully, collect all of the peanuts in a bowl or basket.

4. Have the students sit in a circle (on the floor works best). Begin passing one peanut at a time around the circle. As the students recognize their peanuts, have them hold onto them. As most of the peanuts are claimed, there may be some students who still do not recognize their peanuts. Give students a chance to verbalize the features of their peanuts. Some students may need to recheck the peanuts they have claimed as you get to the last few peanuts.

5. Discuss this activity with the students. Point out the uniqueness of each peanut that made it easily recognizable. Make a connection between unique peanuts and unique people. Even though there are millions of people (peanuts) in the world, each one is unique. Point out that if this uniqueness is true of peanuts that have no ability to individuate, imagine how much more true it is of people who have the ability to grow and change and bring their own personalities into everything they do.

Teacher Tip:

This activity could also be done with dried beans, feathers, oranges, etc.

Extensions:

After your students have examined the peanuts, collect them and return them for identification the following day. Try returning them after four days. Ask your students to notice the difference in their ability to recognize their peanuts.

Bloom's Taxonomy

Knowledge

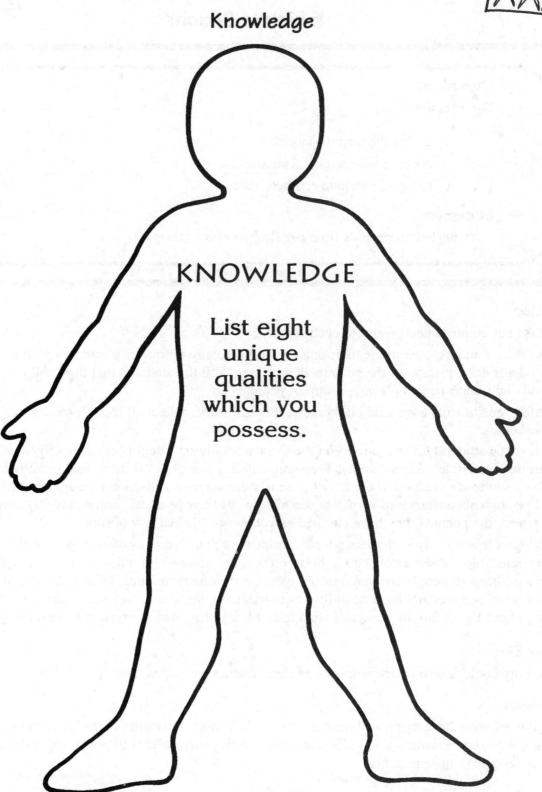

KNOWLEDGE

List eight unique qualities which you possess.

Teacher's Directions: Copy this page onto construction paper or card stock. Cut out and laminate the shape. Post the activity in a center for student use or used as seat work by individual students.

Bloom's Taxonomy

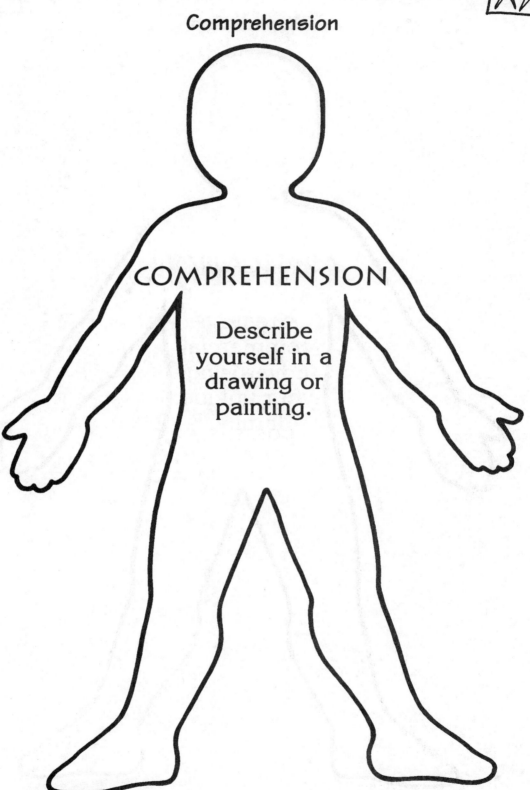

Comprehension

COMPREHENSION

Describe yourself in a drawing or painting.

Teacher's Directions: Copy this page onto construction paper or card stock. Cut out and laminate the shape. Post this activity in a center for student use or used as seat work by individual students.

Bloom's Taxonomy

Application

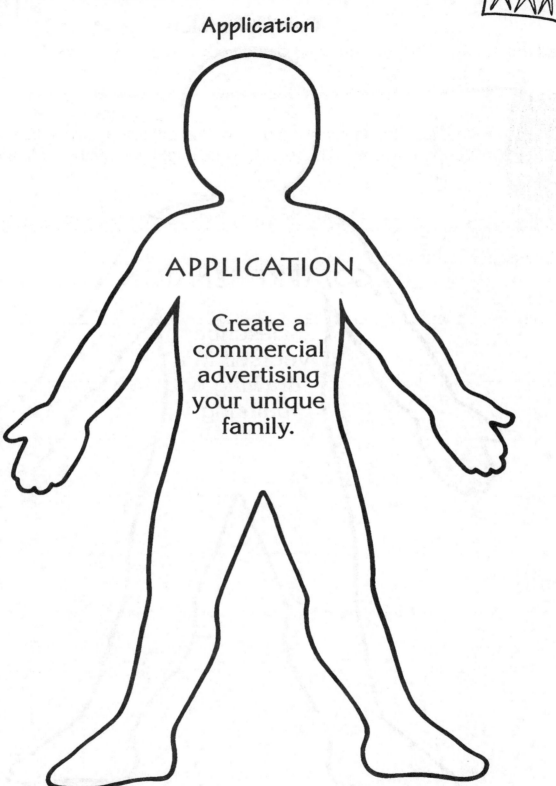

APPLICATION

Create a
commercial
advertising
your unique
family.

Teacher's Directions: Copy this page onto construction paper or card stock. Cut out and laminate the shape. Post this activity in a center for student use or used as seat work by individual students.

Problem Solving

Activity #1

Read the situation below and write down your ideas.

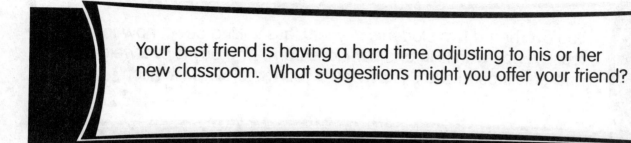

Your best friend is having a hard time adjusting to his or her new classroom. What suggestions might you offer your friend?

Write your ideas here:

_____

_____

_____

_____

_____

_____

_____

_____

_____

_____

Problem Solving

Activity #2

Read the situation below and write down your ideas.

> You overheard two students in your class talking about how to tease a boy who is in another classroom. The boy is overweight and gets teased a lot. How would you handle this situation?

Write your ideas here:

_____

_____

_____

_____

_____

_____

_____

_____

_____

Problem Solving

Activity #3

Read the situation below and write down your ideas.

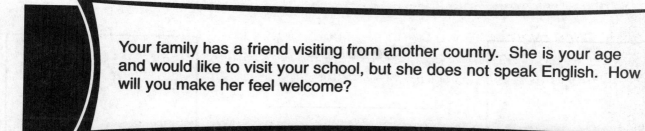

Your family has a friend visiting from another country. She is your age and would like to visit your school, but she does not speak English. How will you make her feel welcome?

Write your ideas here:

_____

_____

_____

_____

_____

_____

_____

_____

Connections Activity

How Are They Connected?

because

_____

_____

_____

because   **because**

_____   _____

_____   _____

_____   _____

Teacher's Directions: Use this page as a culminating activity. Assess your students' understanding of the information taught in the "People" unit, explore and debate issues, or increase flexible thinking in relation to the people topic. You may wish to make related vocabulary words available for your students to use. This page is designed to encourage your students to explore and expand their concepts of making connections.

Overview of Environment Centers

Focus Topic: Environments Require Care

Objectives

Students will . . .

 . . . identify endangered species.

 . . . identify life forms dependent on the environment.

 . . . identify a variety of environmental elements.

 . . . recognize human kind's impact on the environment.

 . . . understand concepts of environmental misuse.

 . . . make recommendations for the care of the environment.

 . . . recognize pollution as having a negative impact.

Center Activities

On the blank lines write the names of the centers in which you plan to locate each activity.

Center #1 _____

Activity A—Endangered Species: Using an activity sheet and flash cards, students will gather and report information about endangered species.

Activity B—Masks: Students will create and color animal masks.

Center #2 _____

Activity A—My Environment: Students will draw an environment in which they spend time each day.

Activity B—Shaping the Environment: With clay on a paper plate base, students will create and identify at least five different physical landforms.

Center #3 _____

Activity A—People and the Environment: Students will create environmentally pro-active posters.

Activity B—Pitch In!: Using bags and art materials, students will create trash bags with environmental messages.

Center #4 _____

Activity A—Growing Beans: Students will plant and chart the growth of the lima beans.

Activity B—Plants, Plants, Plants!: Using a plant parts activity sheet, students will cut and paste to create a unique, flowering plant.

Center #5_____

Activity A—Pollution in Our Environment: Students will search for information and create a trash can fact pack.

Activity B—Home Sweet Home: Students will assemble a nature cover-up picture, using an activity sheet and crayons.

There are two activities for each center in this unit. The first set of centers can be planned on this page. The second set of activities is on the next page. On the blank lines write the names of the centers in which you plan to locate each activity.

Environment Center Planner—Part One

Environments Require Care

1. _____	2. _____	3. _____	4. _____	5. _____
Endangered Species: Gather and report information about endangered species.	**My Environment:** Draw an environment.	**People and the Environment:** Create environmentally pro-active posters.	**Growing Beans:** Observe and chart the growth of a lima bean.	**Pollution in Our Environment:** Search for information and create a trash can fact pack.

Materials

Plans

Notes

Use this chart to plan the second set of activities for your centers in this unit. On the blank lines write the names of the centers in which you plan to locate each activity.

Environment Centers Planner—Part Two

Environments Require Care

1. _____	2. _____	3. _____	4. _____	5. _____
Masks: Create and color animal masks.	**Shaping the Environment:** Create landforms using clay.	**Pitch In!:** Create a usable garbage bag with a message.	**Plants, Plants, Plants!:** Cut and paste to make a unique flowering plant.	**Home Sweet Home!:** Assemble a nature cover-up picture.

Materials

Plans

Notes

Center #1: Activity A

Endangered Species

Objectives:

Students will . . .

. . . understand the term "endangered."

. . . recognize species which are endangered.

. . . gather information about endangered species.

. . . present information on an activity sheet.

Materials:

❋ 2 or 3 copies of page 37, laminated and cut into puzzle pieces for the center

❋ a copy of the activity sheet on page 38 for each student

❋ a copy of the answer sheet (page 39) for the center

Activity:

Depending on your students' level of exposure, you may need to introduce and/or define the term *endangered*. Be sure to discuss and differentiate among the terms *threatened, endangered,* and *extinct*. Provide as much information as possible on endangered species in the center (e.g., posters, puzzles, books, pictures, and flash cards). Copy endangered species puzzle onto heavy paper, laminate, and cut into pieces. Students may put puzzle pieces together to discover the answers. Have your students use the puzzle and other center resources to complete an activity sheet.

Teacher Tips:

It is helpful to pull in all available resources (of which there are many) about endangered species. Check local learning stores, bookstores, and libraries for information. Use software, videos, posters, and animal models to augment your center.

Extensions:

Have students choose an animal to report on. Take a field trip to a local animal reserve or zoo. If you go to a zoo be sure to discuss the pros and cons of zoos (e.g., Pros . . . animals are safe and people become educated. Cons . . . animals live out of their true habitats and lack freedom).

Student Directions Card:

Put together the Endangered Species Puzzle. Use the facts on the puzzle and any other resources to complete the Endangered Species Activity Sheet.

Center #1: Activity A

Endangered Species Puzzle

Teacher's Directions: Make several copies of this page. Laminate the copies and cut the puzzles along the dotted lines. Place the puzzle pieces in envelopes.

Endangered Species Puzzle

1. Giant pandas are chubby mammals that live in a few remote regions of China.

2. Most of the crocodiles left in the U.S. live in the Everglades.

3. Wolves travel in packs of two to eight.

4. The biggest problem manatees face is boats.

5. Gorillas live in the mountain jungles of Africa.

6. Nene geese are different from other geese because they do not like water and do not migrate.

7. Elephant tusks are made of ivory.

8. Kangaroos stick together in groups called mobs.

9. The aye-aye is a member of a family of long-tailed noisy animals called Lemurs.

10. Rhinoceros horns were once used for powdered medicine and knife handles.

Center #1: Activity A

Endangered Species Activity Sheet

Fill in the blanks.

1. Giant pandas are chubby mammals that live in a few remote regions of

   _____.

2. Most of the crocodiles left in the U.S. live in the_____.

3. Wolves travel in packs of _____.

4. The biggest problem manatees face is _____.

5. Gorillas live in the mountain jungles of _____.

6. Nene geese are different from other geese because_____

   _____ and _____.

7. Elephant tusks are made of

   _____.

8. Kangaroos stick together in groups called

   _____.

9. The aye-aye is a member of a family of

   long-tailed noisy animals called

   _____.

10. Rhinoceros horns were once used for

    _____

    _____

    and _____.

Center #1: Activity A

Endangered Species Answer Key

1. China

2. Everglades

3. two to eight

4. boats

5. Africa

6. they do not like water;
   they do not migrate

7. ivory

8. mobs

9. Lemurs

10. powdered medicine;
    knife handles

Center #1: Activity B

Masks

Objectives:

Students will . . .

. . . use animal outlines to create masks.

. . . use realistic markings to color animals.

Materials:

* animal outline
* animal posters or pictures which show actual colors and markings
* white construction paper
* string
* markers

Activity:

Have each of your students choose an animal outline to make into a mask. Tell your students to cut and color their masks. Strings can be attached to hold the masks on.

Teacher Tips:

Use heavy paper or card stock onto which students can trace masks. Be sure that the masks are sturdy. Before punching holes for the strings, place small pieces of tape over the area to be punched.

Extensions:

Students can use the masks to present a skit encouraging animal protection. The masks can be coded to show information (e.g., put two stripes if the animal is a mammal, three dots if it is larger than a child, zigzags if it is an omnivore). Ask your students to imagine that they are actually the animals and write paragraphs describing their lives. The masks can be displayed in hallways or around the classroom door.

Student Directions Card:

Choose an animal outline to make into a mask.

Color your mask as realistically as you can.

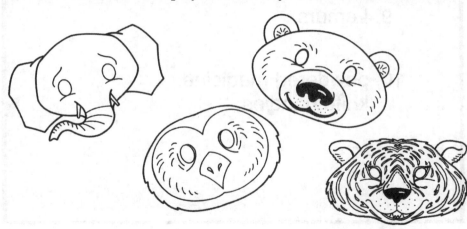

Center #1: Activity B

Bear Mask

Color this mask as realistically as possible. Cut it out, punch holes in the sides, and tie strings to the holes.

Owl Mask

Color this mask as realistically as possible. Cut it out, punch holes in the sides, and tie strings to the holes.

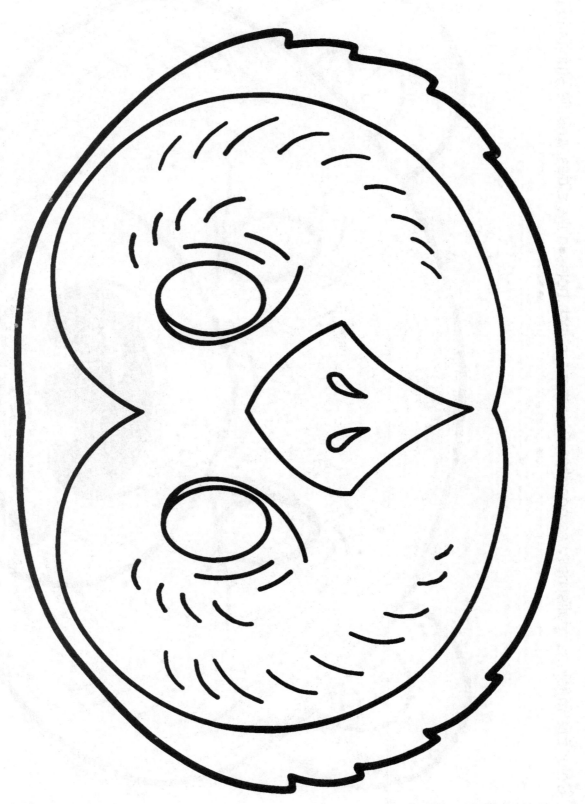

Center #1: Activity B

Tiger Mask

Color this mask as realistically as possible. Cut it out, punch holes in the sides, and tie strings to the holes.

Elephant Mask

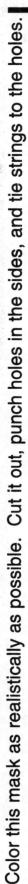

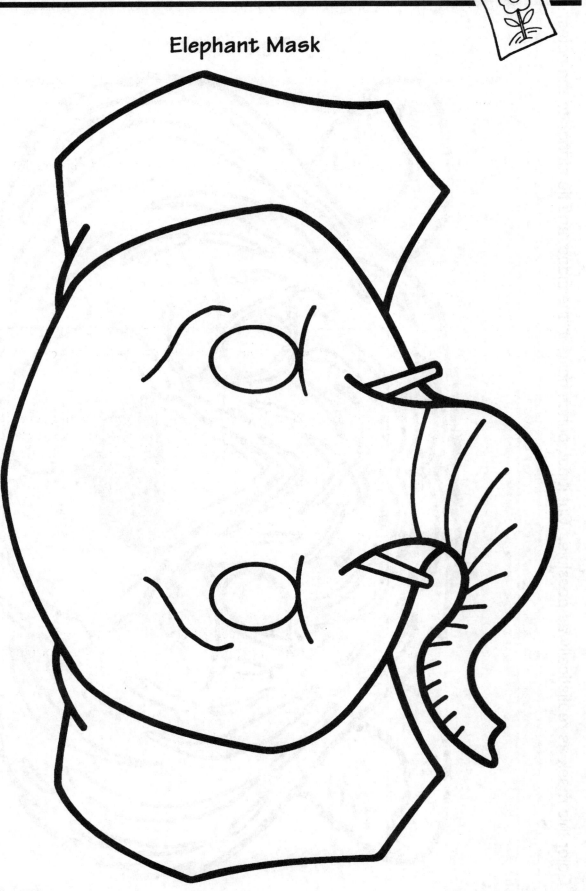

Center #2: Activity A

My Environment

Objectives:

Students will . . .

    . . . recognize different types of environments (natural and man-made).

    . . . draw man-made environments in which they spend time each day.

Materials:

❋ a copy of the window outline (page 46) for each student

❋ markers

Activity:

Use this opportunity to discuss and define the word *environment* (the surrounding conditions). Include in your discussion a variety of environments (city, rural, desert, ocean) and micro-environments (home, school, church, hospital). Encourage students to identify the environments in which they spend time each day. Have the students each draw an environment on a window paper.

Teacher Tips:

Try to have an area for displaying the windows. Discussions will naturally occur among the students as they compare the windows.

Extensions:

Choose three or four windows to compare and contrast. Place the windows on the board. Encourage your students to notice the similarities and differences. Have your students use crayons to draw their window environments and then use construction paper to add shutters, curtains, or other trims.

Student Directions Card:

Pretend that you are looking through a window at a man-made environment in which you spend some of your time each day. Draw this environment within the window outline.

Center #2: Activity A

Window Activity Sheet

Center #2: Activity B

Shaping the Environment

Objectives:

Students will . . .

. . . be able to identify physical landforms.

. . . create an environment out of clay, depicting at least five different landforms.

Materials:

* ❋ copies of pages 48 and 49 for each student
* ❋ a few copies of page 50 to use for reference
* ❋ paper plates
* ❋ clay
* ❋ permanent markers

Activity:

Discuss and define the words on pages 48 and 49. (**Note:** The definition sheets can be completed as a class, in small groups, or by individuals. Students can be responsible for all or part of the definitions.) Post one or two complete definition lists (page 50) in the center for use as a student reference. Have each student use a paper plate and clay to make a landform model. (Markers can be used to color on the clay.) Encourage your students to include five to seven different landforms. Each student should list the landforms on a piece of paper which can be taped to the bottom of the paper plates.

Teacher Tips:

After your students have defined the landform words, discuss the definitions. Also, share pictures of the different types of landforms with your students.

Use sturdy paper plates and modeling clay. Demonstrate to your students the process of smearing clay onto a plate to form oceans, waterways, and flat landforms. Higher landforms can then be added. Toothpicks and masking tape tags can be used to label the landforms.

Extension:

Using a map, have your students locate and label various landforms.

Student Directions Card:

Using a paper plate as your base, create an environment out of clay. Include at least five different landforms in your environment.

Center #2: Activity B

Landform Word List—Part One

Write a definition for each word.

archipelago _____

_____

bay _____

_____

butte _____

_____

canal _____

_____

cape _____

_____

channel _____

_____

delta _____

_____

desert _____

_____

dune _____

_____

glacier _____

_____

gulf _____

_____

harbor _____

_____

Center #2: Activity B

Landform Word List—Part Two

Write a definition for each word.

island _____

_____

isthmus _____

_____

lagoon _____

_____

mesa _____

_____

oasis _____

_____

peninsula _____

_____

plateau _____

_____

reservoir _____

_____

river mouth _____

_____

strait _____

_____

tributary _____

_____

volcano _____

_____

Center #2: Activity B

Landform Definitions

archipelago—a large group of islands

bay—a body of water partly enclosed by land but with a wide outlet to the sea

butte—a hill that rises abruptly from the surrounding area but has sloping sides and a flat top

canal—a man-made waterway or an artificially improved river used for irrigation, shipping, or travel

cape—a point or head of land projecting into a sea or other body of water

channel—the bed of a stream or river; deeper part of a river or harbor, especially a deep navigable passage

delta—a triangular tract of alluvial land between diverging branches of the mouth of a river, often intersected by other branches (alluvium = sediment deposited by flowing water as in a river, flood plain, or delta)

desert—a dry, barren, often sandy region that for environmental reasons can naturally support little or no plant growth

dune—a hill or ridge of windblown sand

glacier—a huge mass of laterally limited moving ice, originating from compacted snow

gulf—a large area of sea or ocean which partially extends to the land

harbor—a sheltered part of a body of water deep enough to provide anchorage for ships

island—a land mass, especially one smaller than a continent, entirely surrounded by water

isthmus—a narrow strip of land connecting two larger masses of land

lagoon—shallow body of water, especially one separated from sea by sandbars or coral reefs

mesa—a flat-topped elevation with one or more clifflike sides; common in the southwestern United States

oasis—a fertile or green spot in a desert

peninsula—a long projection of land into the water, attached to the mainland by an isthmus

plateau—an elevated and comparatively level expanse of land

reservoir—a body of water collected and saved for future use in a natural or artificial lake

river mouth—the opening or entrance into a river (river—a large natural stream of water emptying into an ocean, a lake, or other bodies of water)

straits—a narrow passage of water joining two larger bodies of water

tributary—a stream or river flowing into a larger stream or river

volcano—a vent in the earth's crust through which molten lava and gases are ejected

Center #3: Activity A

People and the Environment

Objectives:

Students will . . .

> . . . be aware of behaviors which have a negative or positive effect on the environment.
>
> . . . recognize people's impact on the environment.
>
> . . . create a poster encouraging three environmentally positive actions.

Materials:

* sample posters
* large white paper (one for each student)
* markers

Activity:

Discuss with your students the differences between behaviors which positively and negatively affect the environment (recycling, littering, etc.). Tell them that they are each going to make a poster encouraging behaviors which have a positive effect on the environment. Create a poster criteria list as a class (or, this can be teacher generated). The following are possible criteria:

* must have a border
* must use two different sizes of letters
* must include three pictures
* must use more than three colors

Teacher Tips:

When discussing positive and negative behaviors as they relate to the environment, create a class list to post in the room. The students can add to this list as they think of new ideas.

Extensions:

Using posters as a starting point, allow the students to make a commercial. In the commercial the students can present their messages by using visual displays or props. The commercials can be video-taped.

Student Directions Card:

Create a poster encouraging three behaviors which have a positive effect on the environment. Be sure to follow the criteria.

Center #3: Activity B

Pitch In!

Objectives:

Students will . . .

. . . observe and recognize environmental messages.

. . . create trash bags with environmental messages.

. . . participate in a clean-up activity.

Materials:

❈ objects displaying environmental messages

❈ brown paper bags, large or small

❈ markers

Activity:

Show your students several items containing environmental messages (e.g., automobile garbage bags, grocery bags, cardboard boxes). Point out how the messages convey important ideas in a concise way. Help your students think of short, catchy phrases that could be used on their trash bags. After the bags are complete, have the students conduct a class clean-up effort at the school or in the local neighborhood.

Teacher Tips:

Use bags that are blank (large bags without words may be hard to find, but can be made using brown postal paper). Have the students show you the words they plan to use on their bags so that you can check the spelling.

Extensions:

Give trash bags as gifts to be used at home or in the car.

Have a school clean-up event. Provide each classroom with a trash bag made by your students. Choose a day and "clean up!"

Student Directions Card:

Using a large paper bag, create a usable trash bag with an environmental message.

Center #4: Activity A

Growing Beans

Objectives:

Students will . . .

. . . understand the process of growth.

. . . recognize the stages of a bean's growth.

. . . plant a bean and monitor its growth.

Materials:

❋ lima beans (one for each student)

❋ small paper cups (one for each student)

❋ a large tray (or two) for the cups to drain on

❋ soil

❋ plant food

❋ index cards

Activity:

Discuss the stages and signs of growth (show pictures if available). Then discuss the elements needed to ensure plant growth—water, sunlight, and food. Talk about the food produced in the seed coat of a bean. Have each student wrap a dry lima bean in a moist paper towel until it sprouts. Beans can be kept in small paper cups labeled with students' names. After the beans sprout, ask the students to draw their beans and the sprouts. Next, have the students plant their beans, in soil, in their paper cups after poking holes in the bottoms. Demonstrate how growth will be recorded on an index card: Day 1—bean planted, Day 2—growth under soil, Day 5—tiny green sprout appears, Day 7— sprout ½ inch (1.3 cm) tall.

Teacher Tips:

Start a few beans ahead of your students so that you can show them what to expect along the way. Soak and plant extra beans so that you will have spare beans at each stage of growth since some beans will not sprout and will need to be replaced.

Show pictures and/or drawings of what the students will see when their beans sprout.

Use waxed cups for planting beans. Paper cups will deteriorate too quickly. Be sure to use a tray under the cups. Have your students check the beans every day.

Extensions:

Try growing other seeds. Start a garden at school. Beautify your school by planting bulbs in the fall to enjoy in the spring.

Student Directions Card:

Plant a bean. Record its daily growth on an index card. Be sure to water your bean plant.

Center #4: Activity B

Plants, Plants, Plants!

Objectives:

Students will . . .

> . . . recognize the parts of a flowering plant.
> . . . create unique flowering plants.
> . . . label the parts of their plants.

Materials:

* ❋ copies of page 55 on various colors of construction paper (one for each student plus extras)
* ❋ extra construction paper or plain white paper to use as backgrounds to the flowers
* ❋ scissors
* ❋ glue

Activity:

Discuss the parts of a flowering plant and the elements that plants need to have to grow. Have students create a unique flowering plant, using the activity sheet on page 55. Stress to your students that all of the plants will be unique creations and that there is no wrong way to put the plants together.

Teacher Tips:

Copy the Plant Parts Activity Sheet on various colors of construction paper. Your students may wish to choose plant parts from among differently colored sheets. Have a box or basket for storing the activity sheets that have been partially used. Be sure to have a resource with labeled plant parts available for your students to use.

Extensions:

Create a large plant by having small groups of students donate plant parts. Play a guessing game by describing the functions of plant parts while the students guess which parts you are describing.

Student Directions Card:

Using the Plant Parts Activity Sheet, create a unique flowering plant. Glue your plant to a plain sheet of paper. Label all of the parts.

Center #4: Activity B

Plant Parts Activity Sheet

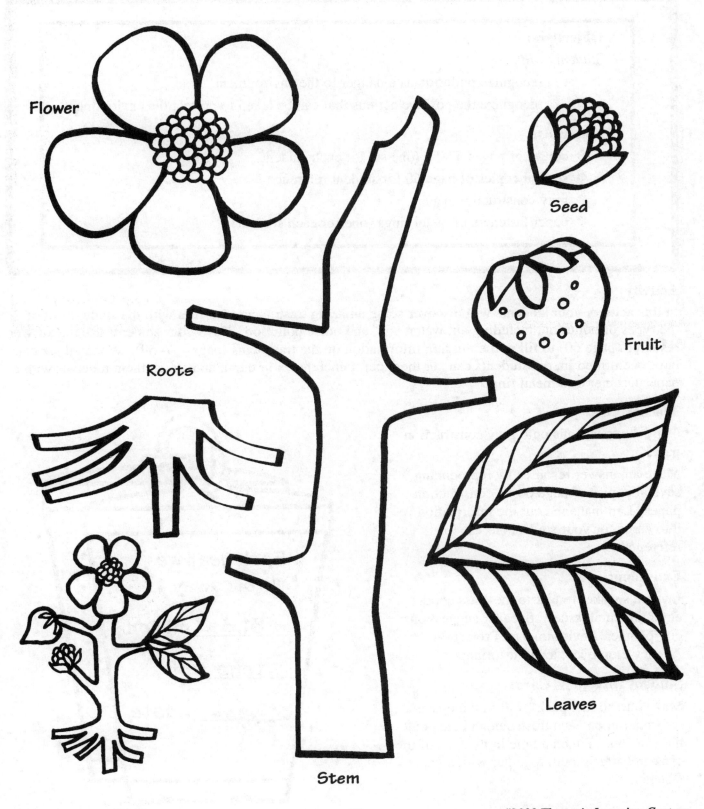

Flower

Seed

Roots

Fruit

Leaves

Stem

Center #5: Activity A

Pollution in Our Environment

Objectives:

Students will . . .

    . . . recognize pollution as a danger to the environment.

    . . . recognize the positive actions that can be taken to protect the environment.

Materials:

* ❋ copies of pages 57–59 (one set for each student)
* ❋ several copies of page 60 for student reference
* ❋ gray construction paper
* ❋ paper fasteners or metal rings (one for each student)

Activity:

In this activity your students will discover some amazing trash facts. Discuss with the students all of the types of pollution, including air, water, soil, and noise pollution. Have your students use the answer resource (page 60) to fill in the missing information on the trash cans (pages 57–59). When all six cans have been filled in, the students can cut them out, punch holes in them, and attach them together with a paper fastener or a metal ring.

Teacher Tips:

Copy the trash cans onto gray construction paper.

Make an answer resource by reproducing several copies of page 60 on construction paper. Laminate and cut the information into cards for your students to use for reference.

Extension:

Invite a speaker to talk to the class about environmental issues. Speaker suggestions: city planner, Environmental Protection Agency employee, local historian.

Student Directions Card:

Make a trash fact pack! Fill in the missing information on each trash can and then cut the cans out. Punch a hole in the tops of the cans and attach them together with a paper fastener.

Each year we throw away ___31.6___ million ___tons___ of ___yard___ waste.

Center #5: Activity A

Trash Can Cutouts

We throw away enough _____ and jars to fill the _____(411 m) _____towers of New York's World _____Center in just _____weeks.

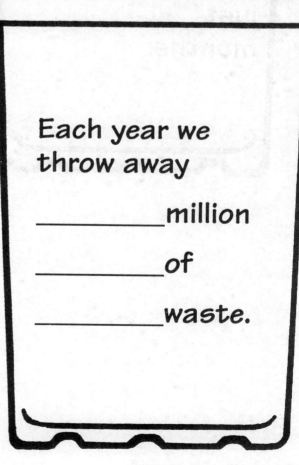

Each year we throw away

_____million

_____of

_____waste.

Center #5: Activity A

Trash Can Cutouts

The United States could _____ its entire commercial _____ with the aluminum we waste in just _____ months.

Every year we throw away _____ billion plastic bottles, and every day we throw away _____ million bottles.

Trash Can Cutouts *(cont.)*

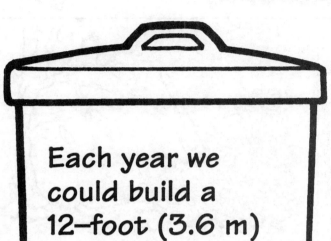

Each year we could build a 12–foot (3.6 m) high wall from

_____ to

_____

_____City, using wasted writing and office paper.

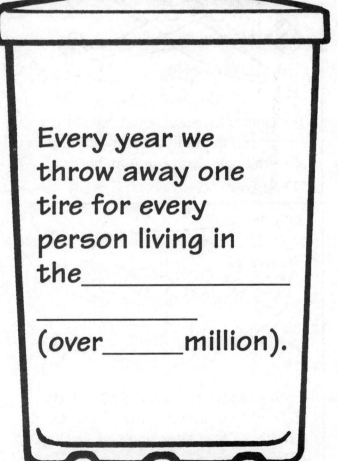

Every year we throw away one tire for every person living in the_____

_____

(over_____million).

Trash Can Information Sheet

We throw away enough bottles and jars to fill the 1,350 foot (411 m) twin towers of New York's World Trade Center in just two weeks.

Each year we throw away 31.6 million tons of yard waste.

The United States could rebuild its entire commercial airfleet with the aluminum we waste in just three months.

Every year we throw away 22 billion plastic bottles, and every day we throw away 2.5 million bottles.

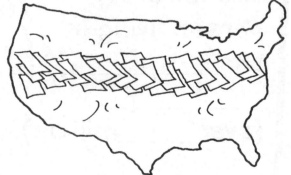

Each year, we could build a 12–foot (3.6 m) high wall from Los Angeles to New York City, using wasted writing and office paper.

Every year we throw away one tire for every person living in the United States (over 200 million).

Center #5: Activity B

Home Sweet Home!

Objectives:

Students will . . .

. . . recognize that plants and trees can be homes to many animals.

Materials:

* ❀ copies of pages 62 and 63 (one set for each student)
* ❀ markers and/or crayons
* ❀ scissors
* ❀ glue

Activity:

Discuss with your students how plants and trees are often used as homes to many animals. Have your students imagine themselves as small creatures, such as squirrels, bugs, and birds. Ask them to imagine finding a safe and protected home. Encourage your students to recognize that the human perspective is only one of many. Demonstrate how the students will assemble the activity sheets.

Teacher Tips:

Copy the cover-up sheets on white construction paper. You may want to use an art knife to pre-cut the openings on the top sheet.

Extensions:

Have your students make cover-up projects of their own. Cover-up sheets can be made for any hidden environment. To make cover-up projects your students will need to first create the top sheet. Next, have students cut the openings. Then they can draw pictures behind the openings to create the second sheet.

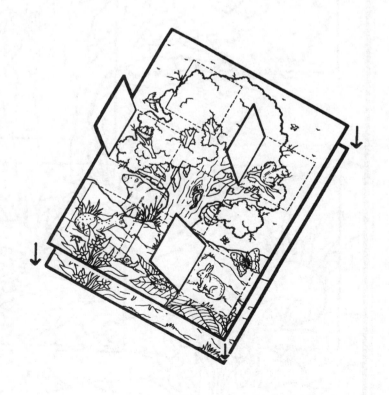

Student Directions Card:

Color and cut the nature Cover-Up Activity Sheets. Assemble this project by gluing the first sheet over the second. Do not glue the windows shut!

Cover-Up Activity Sheet One

Cover-Up Activity Sheet Two

Daily Lesson Plan #1

Rain Power

Objectives:

Students will . . .

    . . . understand the interactions between soil and rain.

    . . . discuss the impact of the rain on soil.

    . . . recognize the implications of the above impact.

    . . . understand the term *splash erosion*.

Materials:

- approximately 15 milk cartons (half-gallon size)
- several rocks
- construction paper to cover the cartons
- permanent markers
- copies of page 65 (one for each student)
- measuring sticks (i.e., yard sticks, meter sticks, rulers)

Activities:

Note: Plan to set up this activity the day before a forecasted rain.

1. Give every two or three students a clean, dry half-gallon milk or juice carton to share. Have the pairs or groups cover the cartons with white construction paper to create splash boards. Assign each carton a number and ask the students to write the numbers on their cartons.

2. Allow your students to place the cartons outside in a variety of areas, such as in a dirt area, on the grass, under trees, and near a building. (Place a rock inside of each carton to hold it in place.)

3. When placing the cartons, have students note the compass orientations on the sides of the cartons with permanent markers.

4. Have your students make hypotheses about how high the rain will splash.

5. After the rain has passed, take a walk to observe the splash boards. Ask the students to measure the heights of the splash marks and then for each fill in an Observation Record (page 65).

6. Have your students formulate some conclusions.

Teacher Tips:

Try making a splash board ahead of time to be sure of your technique. Locate suitable placement areas ahead of time. Guide a student discussion to clarify why rain power is an important environmental consideration (e.g., soil displacement, seed transportation, root exposure, erosion, mud slides).

Extensions:

Do further research by moving the splash boards to new locations. Ask your students to place the splash boards at home and report on their results to the class.

Daily Lesson Plan #1

Observation Record

Record your observations.

Carton Number	Location	Height of Splash	Direction

Daily Lesson Plan #2

Homes: High, Middle, and Low

Objectives:

Students will . . .

    . . . understand that living things live in many different homes and places.

    . . . identify specific homes.

    . . . differentiate animal homes.

    . . . explore the adaptations of specific habitats.

    . . . consider the impact of man on specific homes.

Materials:

- ❖ copies of pages 67 and 68 cut into labels and cards (enough sets for every student or every pair of students)
- ❖ a large piece of construction paper (one for each student or pair of students)
- ❖ scissors
- ❖ glue

Activities:

1. Ask your students to divide up their pieces of construction paper into three equal sections. Then, have them glue one label ("High," "Middle," or "Low") to each section.

2. Using the cards labeled with types of homes and animals (pages 67 and 68), your students can next pair homes with their animals.

3. Next, the students will categorize the locations of homes by placing their pairs in the appropriate sections of their construction paper. For example, a groundhog who lives underground would be placed in the section labeled "Low."

4. Finally, each student can choose a level (high, middle, low) and discuss the possible threats to the homes in that level.

Teacher Tips:

Copy the home and animal cards onto construction paper, laminate, and then cut them into individual cards.

Instead of using the construction paper backgrounds, present the cards to your students as a whole-class bulletin board or wall activity.

Have your students create a chart on paper to show their answers.

Extension:

Challenge your students to choose an animal and report on the status of its home. Include such aspects as threats (such as contamination), loss of environment, and human disruption.

Daily Lesson Plan #2

Animals and Homes

High

Middle

Low

tree	![tree]	squirrel	![squirrel]
underground	![underground]	groundhog	![groundhog]
den	![den]	fox	![fox]
ocean	![ocean]	jellyfish	![jellyfish]

Daily Lesson Plan #2

Animals and Homes (cont.)

pond		**duck**	
grass		**snake**	
trailer		**person**	
doghouse		**dog**	
barn		**horse**	
bush		**caterpillar**	
hive		**bee**	
large nest		**eagle**	
small nest		**hummingbird**	
tunnel		**mole**	

Daily Lesson Plan #3

How Do I Feel?

Objectives:

Students will . . .

> . . . use touch to explore selected objects from nature.
>
> . . . become aware of the textures of objects.
>
> . . . discover word power in describing (use of adjectives).
>
> . . . explore the environment to search for living things.

Materials:

❖ objects collected from outside

Activities:

1. Tell your students to go outside in groups of three to collect samples of living or once-living things.

2. After some objects have been collected, sit in a circle with your students and pass the objects around, one at a time, behind your backs. Have each student describe the object by using one word (an adjective). Encourage your students to use words which have not already been used. Show the object after everyone has had a chance to share.

3. Begin with a new object.

Teacher Tips:

Be sure to clearly define the guidelines for choosing the items. *Do not* let the students pick flowers or leaves. Encourage them to find living things (that will not be harmed by a brief trip indoors) or once living things.

Extensions:

Use the collected items for an art project.

Place the items in a mystery box for students to guess by feeling.

Daily Lesson Plan #4

Earth Management

Objectives:

Students will . . .

    . . . understand the management of the earth.

    . . . explore environmental use and abuse.

    . . . discover the need for compatible protecting and conserving practices in the maintenance of a particular environment.

Materials:

- ❖ large box (for example, a refrigerator box)
- ❖ several pillows
- ❖ markers

Activities:

1. Use a large box (large enough to hold three or four students) to represent the earth. Have your students decorate the box. Place several pillows inside of the box. (Be sure that the box is not too sturdy, as some repair work will enhance the activity.)

2. Brainstorm with your students some classroom uses for the box, such as reading, math, visiting, or reward time.

3. Determine the following through group consensus:

   How often will it be used?

   How will its use be determined?

   How will it be cared for or protected from damage?

4. The box can be used for any length of time. Help your students make connections between the box "earth" management issues and actual environmental management issues.

Teacher Tips:

Be sure your students spend ample time preparing the box for use. This will give them a sense of ownership.

Explain the process of group consensus before engaging in it to avoid disappointments.

Extension:

Have your students write recommendations for earth management, based on their experiences.

Bloom's Taxonomy

Knowledge

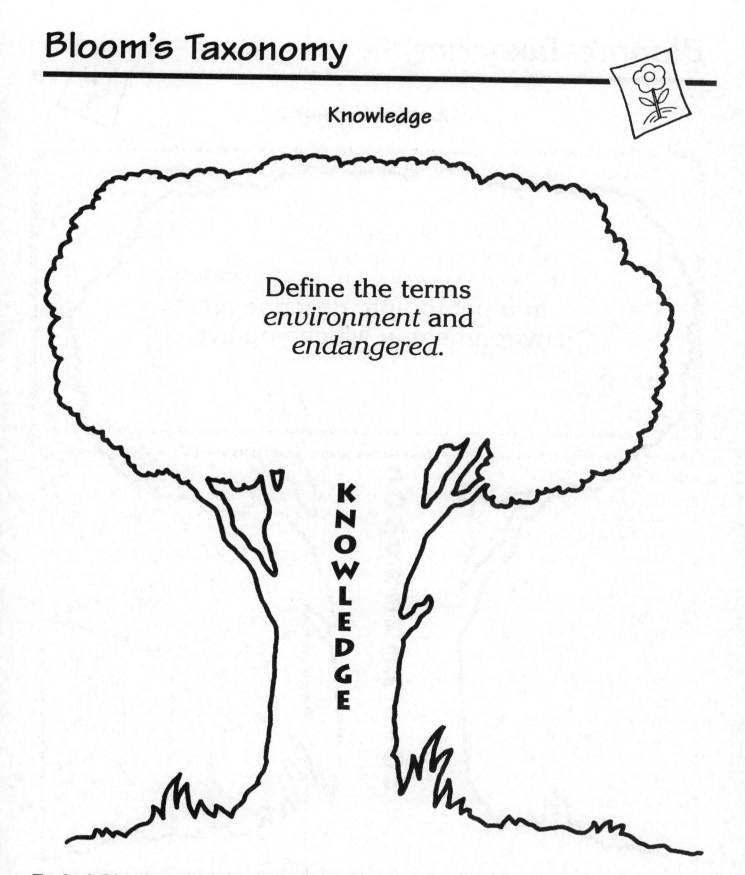

Define the terms
environment and
endangered.

KNOWLEDGE

Teacher's Directions: Copy this page onto construction paper or card stock. Cut out and laminate the shape. This activity can be posted in a center for student use or used as seat work by individual students.

Bloom's Taxonomy

Comprehension

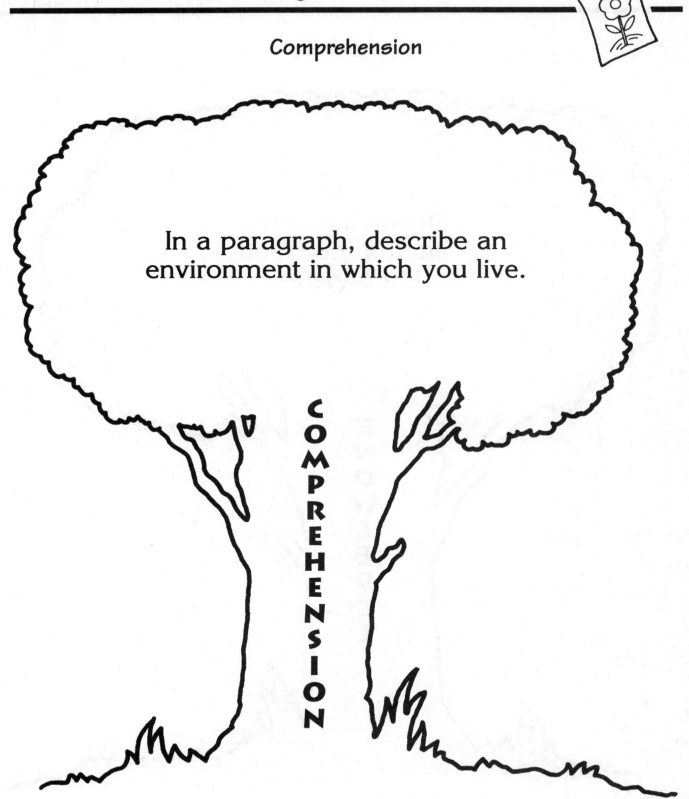

In a paragraph, describe an environment in which you live.

COMPREHENSION

Teacher's Directions: Copy this page onto construction paper or card stock. Cut out and laminate the shape. This activity can be posted in a center for student use or used as seat work by individual students.

Bloom's Taxonomy

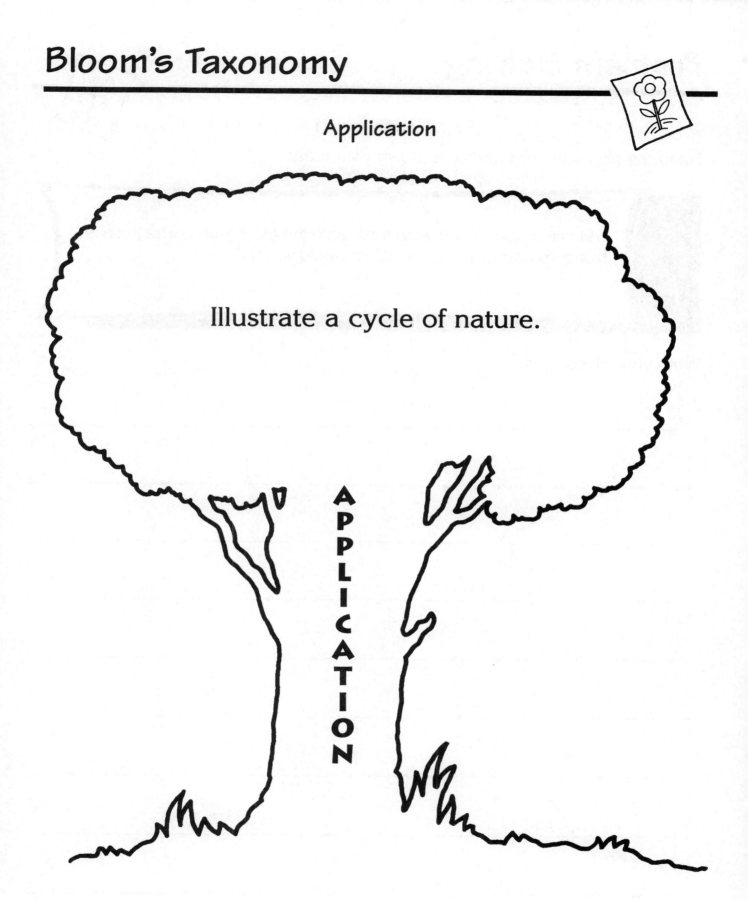

Application

Illustrate a cycle of nature.

APPLICATION

Teacher's Directions: Copy this page onto construction paper or card stock. Cut out and laminate the shape. This activity can be posted in a center for student use or used as seat work by individual students.

Problem Solving

Activity #1

Read the situation card and write down your ideas.

You see a student throwing trash onto the playground. The trash is being spread by the wind. What would you do?

Write your ideas here:

_____

_____

_____

_____

_____

_____

_____

_____

Problem Solving

Activity #2

Read the situation card and write down your ideas.

A large area of trees is scheduled to be cut down to make a parking lot for a local store. What three reasons could you offer for not cutting down the trees? What two alternative plans could you suggest?

Write your ideas here:

_____

_____

_____

_____

_____

_____

_____

_____

_____

Problem Solving

Activity #3

Read the situation card and write down your ideas.

You see an animal at the zoo repeatedly getting teased and harassed. If you were a zoo owner, how would you protect this animal and educate the public at the same time?

Write your ideas here:

_____

_____

_____

_____

_____

_____

_____

_____

Connections Activity

Environments

How Are They Connected?

because

_____

_____

_____

_____

because   **because**

_____   _____

_____   _____

_____   _____

_____   _____

Teacher's Directions: Use this page as a culminating activity. Assess your students' understanding of the information taught in the "Environment" unit, explore and debate issues, or increase flexible thinking in relation to the environment topic. You may wish to make related vocabulary words available for your students to use. This page is designed to encourage your students to explore and expand their concepts of making connections.

Overview of Community Centers

Focus Topic: Communities Need Cooperation

Objectives

Students will . . .

. . . recognize community as a cooperative effort.

. . . understand community terminology.

. . . experience functions of community members.

. . . operate as a cooperative member of a community.

Center Activities

On the blank lines write the names of the centers in which you plan to locate each activity.

Center #1 _____

Activity A—Passport: Using an activity sheet and a resource, students will define community-related words.

Activity B—My Community: Students will create a map of a community.

Activity C—Community Worker Pictures: On large white paper, students will depict two community jobs.

Center #2 _____

Activity A—Money Maker: Using money outlines, students will design their own currency.

Activity B—Bank It!: Students will record imaginary bank transactions.

Activity C—Logo Maker: Students will create a simple class logo.

Center #3 _____

Activity A—Community Newspaper: Working as a team, students will create a class newspaper.

Activity B—Regional Foods: Students will create recipes, using regional foods.

Activity C—Types of Homes: Students will recognize the many types of homes which make up communities.

Center #4 _____

Activity A—Community Workers: Using community worker cards, students will complete a directory.

Activity B—Job Applications: Students will fill out a job application.

Activity C—Job Search: Using a newspaper as a resource, students will complete a job search questionnaire.

Center #5 _____

Activity A—Building a House: Students will build a house out of a kit.

Activity B—Community Service: Students will engage in a model community service project.

There are three activities for each center (except for center five, which only has two) in this unit. The first set of centers can be planned on this page. The second set of activities are on the next page and the third set is on page 81. On the blank lines write the names of the centers in which you plan to locate each activity.

Community Centers Planner—Part One

Communities Need Cooperation

1. _____	2. _____	3. _____	4. _____	5. _____
Passport: Use activity sheets and a resource to define community related words.	**Money Maker:** Design original currency.	**Community Newspaper:** Create a class newspaper.	**Community Workers:** Complete a directory of community workers.	**Building a House:** Build a house from a kit.

Materials

Plans

Notes

Use this chart to plan the second set of activities for your centers in this unit. On the blank lines write the names of the centers in which you plan to locate each activity.

Community Centers Planner—Part Two

Communities Need Cooperation

1. _____	2. _____	3. _____	4. _____	5. _____
My Community: Create a community map.	**Bank It!:** Record bank transactions.	**Regional Foods:** Concoct a recipe, using a regional food.	**Job Applications:** Fill out a job application.	**Community Service:** Engage in a model community service activity.

Materials

Plans

Notes

Use this chart to plan the third set of activities for your centers in this unit. On the blank lines write the names of the centers in which you plan to locate each activity.

Community Centers Planner—Part Three

Communities Need Cooperation

1. _____	2. _____	3. _____	4. _____
Community Worker Pictures: Depict two community jobs.	**Logo Maker:** Create a simple class logo.	**Types of Homes:** Draw residents of various types of homes.	**Job Search:** Complete a job search questionnaire.

Materials

Plans

Notes

Center #1: Activity A

Passport

Objectives:

Students will . . .

. . . recognize community-related terminology.

Materials:

* ❋ passport
* ❋ definitions for passport
* ❋ passport definition puzzle
* ❋ dictionaries

Activity:

Before making copies of the passport pages, fill in the two blanks at the top of the first page with the name of your town, city, etc. Discuss the community words on pages 83–85. Help your students understand the meanings of the words. Have your students use the passport definition puzzle (pages 86–89) or dictionaries to complete their community passports.

Teacher Tips:

Help the students recognize the importance of understanding the community vocabulary. Use this vocabulary in your presentations and activities. Depending on your students' ability levels, you may want to fill in three to four of the definitions before photocopying the passports for them.

To make the passport puzzles, make copies of pages 86–89 and laminate them. Cut out the pieces around the outside edges and on the dividing lines between the words and the definitions. Store the puzzle sets in baskets for the students to use.

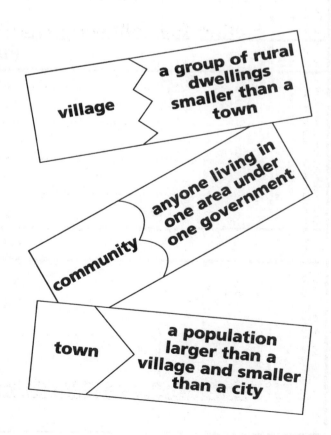

Extensions:

Challenge your students to use the words in sentences.

Use passport words as a class spelling list.

Student Directions Card:

Using a passport definition puzzle or a dictionary, complete a passport.

Center #1: Activity A

Passport Definitions

This is your passport to _____.

Once you have successfully completed this assignment, you will be a citizen of _____.

Every passport has a picture of its owner on it. Draw a picture of yourself below.

Define the following words:

community _____

_____

town _____

_____

village_____

_____

suburb _____

_____

Center #1: Activity A

Passport Definitions *(cont.)*

Define the following words:

urban _____

_____

rural _____

_____

profit_____

_____

city _____

_____

government_____

_____

laws _____

_____

tax _____

_____

consumer _____

_____

Center #1: Activity A

Passport Definitions *(cont.)*

community: anyone living in one area under one government

town: a population larger than a village and smaller than a city

village: a group of rural dwellings smaller than a town

suburb: a residential center in an area outside of a city

urban: anything relating to a city and its environment

rural: having to do with the country

profit: money left over after everything has been paid for

city: a center of population with legal boundaries

government: a single person or a group of people who control public rules and laws

laws: the rules of a community, state, and country

tax: the money paid by the people to support the government

consumer: a person who buys things (or services) from a seller

Our Town ©1995 Zephyr Press Arizona

Passport Puzzle

community ⟩ anyone living in one area under one government

town ⟩ a population larger than a village and smaller than a city

village ⟩ a group of rural dwellings smaller than a town

Passport Puzzle *(cont.)*

suburb | **a residential center in an area outside of a city**

urban | **anything relating to a city and its environment**

rural | **having to do with the countryside**

Passport Puzzle *(cont.)*

profit — **the money left over after everything has been paid for**

city — **a center of population with legal boundaries**

government — **a single person or a group of people who control public rules and laws**

Passport Puzzle (cont.)

laws — **the rules of a community, state, and country**

tax — **the money paid by the people to support the government**

consumer — **a person who buys things (or services) from a seller**

Center #1: Activity B

My Community

Objectives:

Students will . . .

. . . recognize local business and residential areas.

. . . define the local community in map form.

Materials:

* black felt-tip markers
* maps of various communities
* copies of pages 91 and 92
* scissors
* glue
* crayons

Activity:

Ask your students to brainstorm a list of businesses in your local area. Post the list in the center. Discuss maps of various communities and show examples. Maps can include street maps, tourist maps with sights highlighted, and recreational or cartoon maps. After discussing maps and showing several examples, have each of your students draw a map of your community (or an imagined community) on large white paper. They may wish to use some of the building illustrations on the following pages along with their own art or use all of their own illustrations. To use the next two pages, your students can cut out the boxes they need, color them, and paste them to their maps.

Teacher Tips:

Before the students begin their maps, show them how to create lines for major roads.

If you should decide to have your students create maps of imaginary communities, discuss how the buildings might logically be spaced. For example, the houses would be clustered together and the gas station would be on a major road.

If you choose to allow your students to use the illustrations, encourage them to supplement these with their own illustrations of buildings.

Extensions:

Ask your students to create keys to go with their maps.

Have your students make scales for their maps for distance, e.g., 1 inch = 2 miles (2.5 cm = 5 km).

Student Directions Card:

Create a map of your community on a piece of large, white paper. Include local businesses, schools, libraries, parks, etc.

Center #1: Activity B

Community Buildings

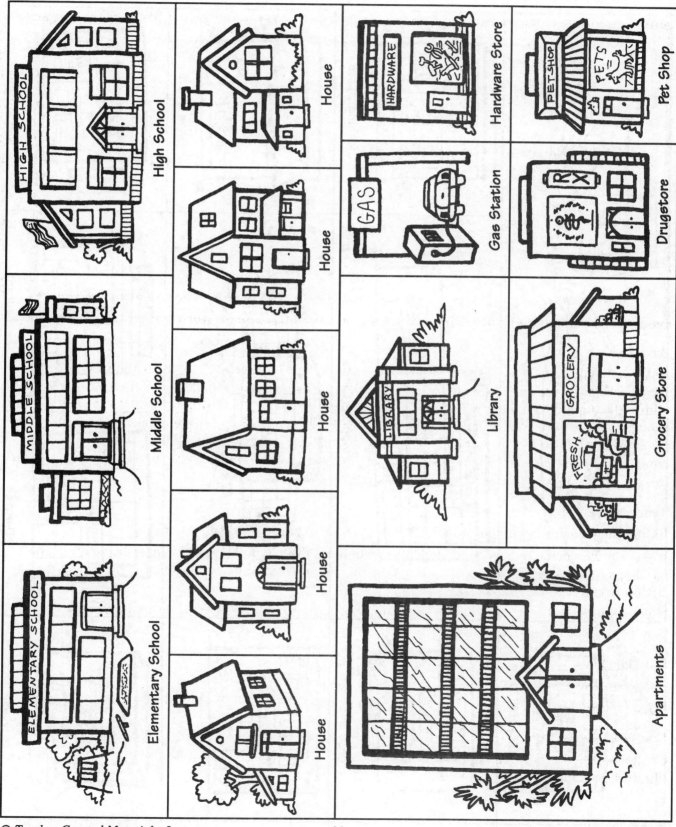

High School

House

Hardware Store

Pet Shop

Middle School

House

Gas Station

Drugstore

Elementary School

House

Library

Grocery Store

House

House

Apartments

Center #1: Activity B

Community Buildings *(cont.)*

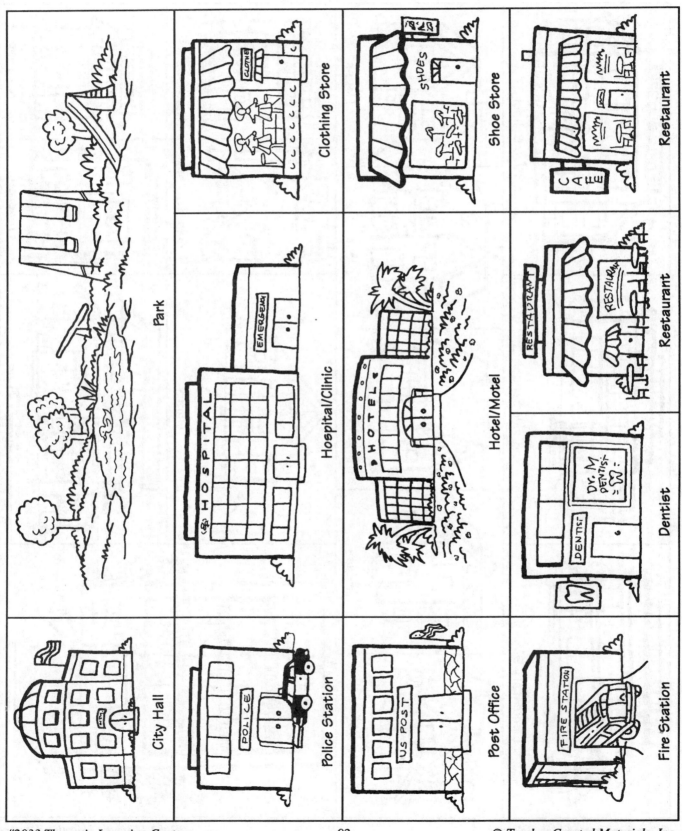

Park

Clothing Store

Shoe Store

Restaurant

Hospital/Clinic

Hotel/Motel

Restaurant

Dentist

City Hall

Police Station

Post Office

Fire Station

Center #1: Activity C

Community Workers Pictures

Objectives:

Students will . . .

    . . . recognize the roles of community workers.

    . . . draw two community workers.

    . . . describe two community workers.

Materials:

❋ a copy of page 94 for each student

❋ crayons

Activity:

Discuss the workers in your community and their roles. Have your students choose two community workers to draw and color on their activity sheets. Below each picture the students will write sentences describing the workers' jobs.

Teacher Tips:

Brainstorm a list of community workers. Post it in the center. Display your students' work. Encourage them to use color and detail.

Extensions:

Make a class book out of the drawings.

Use the community workers drawings as story starters.

Student Directions Card:

Draw a community worker on each side of your activity sheet. Describe each worker's job in two to four sentences.

Center #1: Activity C

People Who Work in My Community

Center #2: Activity A

Money Maker

Objectives:

Students will . . .

    . . . create their own money designs.

    . . . recognize denominations of money.

Materials:

❋ $1, $5, $10 bills (also foreign money, if desired)

❋ a copy of page 96 for each student

❋ fine-point markers, black (or various colors)

❋ scissors

Activity:

Discuss the purposes and uses of money with your students. Ask them to try to think of eight ways in which money is used every day. Show the students several denominations of money and discuss the features on each bill. Have your students create their own money, using copies of the money outlines on page 96.

Teacher Tips:

Be sure to discuss laws against counterfeiting so that your students understand the purpose of this activity.

Extensions:

Use the student-made money for math activities.

Let your students use their money to "buy" classroom privileges.

Student Directions Card:

Use the money outlines to design your own money. Create at least three different denominations.

Center #2: Activity A

Money Outlines

Directions: Create your own money of three different denominations.

Center #2: Activity B

Bank It!

Objectives:

Students will . . .

   . . . understand the purposes and uses of banks.

   . . . use bank account forms to record expenses.

   . . . explore daily expenses.

Materials:

❋ a bank account sheet for each student (page 100)

❋ a copy of of pages 98 and 99

❋ box for expense cards

❋ one transparency copy of page 100

Activity:

Lead a discussion about banks and bank accounts and how they work. Explain how bank accounts can be added to or subtracted from. Using a transparency of the bank account form, demonstrate to your students how to subtract expenses and how to keep a current balance. For the activity, tell your students that they will be drawing expense cards from a box, and subtracting each one from their balances.

To prepare for this activity, laminate and cut out the expense cards. Place them in a box. Also, decide on an appropriate beginning balance for your students. Write this number on the balance sheet in the column entitled "In" (page 100) before making your copies. Explain that you have made a generous deposit into each bank account to get them started.

Teacher Tips:

Depending on your students' ability level, you may want to simplify the form. Do this by covering the information not wanted before copying.

Demonstrate the use of the bank account sheet while the students have one in front of them to fill in as you go along.

Decorate the expense box by gluing advertisements to the outside.

Extensions:

Use the expense cards for whole-group addition or subtraction board activities.

Take a trip to a local bank or have a banker visit the class to discuss accounts.

Student Directions Card:

Draw cards from the expense box. Use the bank account sheet to record your expenses.

Center #2: Activity B

Expense Cards

$50.00 veterinarian bill	$50.00 ski trip	$18.00 amusement park	$6.00 movie
$87.00 auto repair	$15.00 dog food	$2.00 swimming	$9.00 dry cleaning
$90.00 school clothes	$23.00 lawn care	$15.00 pizza party	$6.00 new socks
$5.00 charitable donation	$55.00 club membership	$6.00 parking ticket	$1.00 candy bar

Center #2: Activity B

$10.00 new hat	**$50.00** electricity bill	**$125.00** new bicycle	**$105.00** grocery bill
$20.00 dinner out	**$7.00** tire repair	**$12.00** gasoline	**$18.00** newspaper subscription
$39.00 athletic shoes	**$3.00** telephone call	**$2.00** comic book	**$3.00** cough medicine
$1.00 binder paper	**$2.00** hamburger	**$6.00** birthday gift	**$2.00** ferry ride

Center #2: Activity B

Bank Account Balance Sheet

Directions: Record your expenses.

Date	Expense Description	In	Out	Balance

How many expense cards were you able to draw before going broke? _____

Our Town ©1995 Zephyr Press, Arizona

Center #2: Activity C

Logo Maker

Objectives:

Students will . . .

   . . . understand the elements and purposes of a logo.

   . . . recognize common logos.

   . . . create simple logos.

Materials:

- ❋ several copies of page 102 (for tracing)
- ❋ art tools, such as a T-square, compass, protractor
- ❋ white drawing paper
- ❋ fine-tip, black, felt markers
- ❋ list of criteria to be displayed in the center (for example, logos must have certain dimensions, logos must combine three art elements, logos must include town name)

Activity:

Discuss with your students the purposes and elements of various logos. Show examples from common products. Point out the simple designs of logos. Next, explain that they will each be creating a community logo and discuss what community features should be included (perhaps landscape, name, climate). Ask your students to each sketch four logo ideas on a sheet of paper. (Use one paper divided into four sections by folding or by drawing lines.) Have each student choose one logo to finalize with added art elements, if desired. The final logos should be done on white paper with fine-tip, black, felt markers.

Teacher Tips:

Provide art elements (page 102) for tracing, if desired, to help students get started. However, stress creativity.

Point out that there is no correct answer or logo.

Display all of the logos.

If necessary, discuss appropriate and inappropriate drawings.

Extensions:

Have your students create school logos. Choose one of these logos through a vote. Copy the school logo onto notepaper for the students to use.

Have the students create group or table logos. The logos can then be used to identify groups.

Student Directions Card:

Design a simple logo for your community. Be sure to follow the posted criteria.

Center #2: Activity C

Art Elements

Directions: Use the basic art elements below for tracing or for logo ideas.

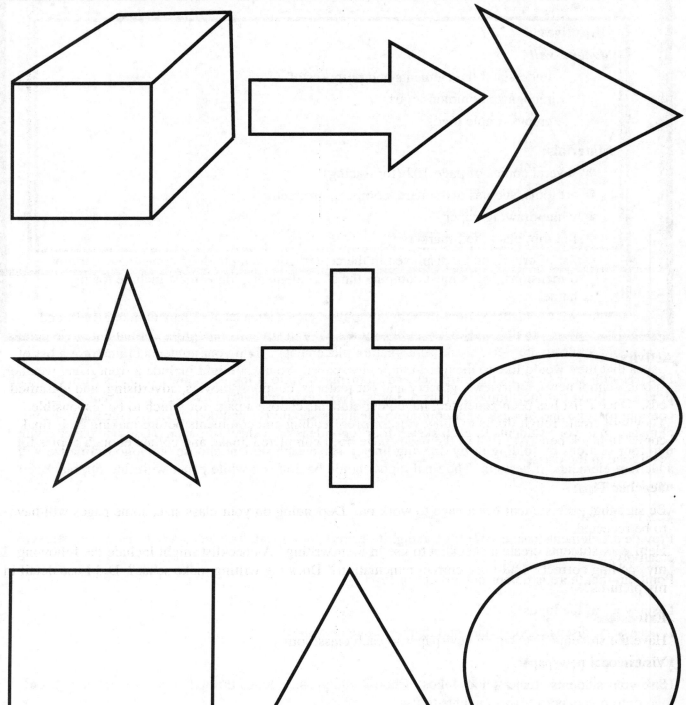

Center #3: Activity A

Community Newspaper

Objectives:

Students will . . .

> . . . cooperate to create a community publication.
>
> . . . prepare copy-ready pages.
>
> . . . use a checklist to review their work.

Materials:

* white paper
* lined paper
* black, felt-tip pens
* checklist to post (generated by the class)

Activity:

Discuss with your students various community publications, such as newspapers, magazines, and pamphlets. Show examples. Review publications, helping students recognize format and style details (e.g., bold lettering, borders, block print, picture placement). Help your students brainstorm a list of pages that they would like to include in their newspaper. Your list might include a front page, weather, sports, school news, interviews, grocery and pet features, coupons, movies, advertising, and classified ads. Once a list has been generated, have your students choose a page for which to be responsible. They will create rough drafts to show you for proofreading and comments before making their final copies in black pen. After all of the pages have been completed, make and collate enough copies for everyone in the class.

Teacher Tips:

Be sure that each student has a page to work on. Depending on your class size, some pages will have to be repeated.

Help your students create a checklist to use in their writing. A checklist might include the following: Is my spelling correct? Did I use correct punctuation? Does my writing make sense? Did I use detail in my pictures?

Extensions:

Have the students distribute a newspaper to each classroom.

Visit a local newspaper.

Subscribe to a newspaper for the class.

Student Directions Card:

Make a rough draft of your newspaper page. After showing it to your teacher, make a final draft in black pen.

Center #3: Activity B

Regional Foods

Objectives:

Students will . . .

. . . recognize regional foods in their community and/or state.

. . . write an original recipe for a regional food.

Materials:

❋ one copy of the activity sheet on page 105 for each student

❋ measuring cups

❋ measuring spoons

Activity:

Discuss with your students the fact that different regions of the country specialize in different types of food. Each area's climate and natural resources dictate what can and cannot grow in that area. Next, as a class, develop a list of several foods that your community and/or state are known for. Post this list in the center for student reference.

Explain to your students that they will be writing a new recipe, using one of these foods. Encourage them to be creative. For example, if your regional food is the apple, instead of an apple pie recipe, create a recipe for apple mustard or apple pizza! Do not worry about how tasty the recipe might actually be. This should simply be an exercise in creativity.

Teacher Tips:

You may wish to display clearly labeled measuring cups and measuring spoons so that your students will be able to easily visualize measurement amounts.

Extension:

Collect the recipes and bind them together into a classroom regional food cookbook.

Student Directions Card:

Write a recipe on the activity sheet. Use one food which is from your community or state.

Regional Recipe

This is a recipe for _____

Center #3: Activity C

Types of Homes

Objectives:

Students will . . .

     . . . recognize the many different types of homes which make up communities, present and past.

     . . . students will draw the people which might inhabit different types of homes.

Materials:

❋ one copy of each activity sheet (pages 107 and 108) for each student

❋ crayons

❋ books for reference

❋ scissors

Activity:

Initiate a discussion with your students about different types of homes. Explain that there are many kinds of shelter around the world and throughout history. Every community must have homes. Often, there is variation even within a community. For example, there may be houses, apartments, and farms in one community.

Show the two activity sheets to your students. Explain that they will be drawing a person who might live, or might have lived, in each home.

Depending on the needs of your students, you may wish to discuss the homes before they start this activity.

Teacher Tips:

Make available resource books which show homes from around the world.

Be sensitive to the living situations of your students. Do they live in houses, apartments, mobile homes, boats, cabins, houseboats, etc.? Ignoring a particular type of home may imply to a child that it is not an accepted, or at least usual, way of living.

Extensions:

Ask your students to each choose and cut out one type of home from the activity sheets. Next, tell them to glue their homes to a blank piece of white paper and draw the appropriate landscapes around the homes.

Student Directions Card:

On the right sides of the activity pages 107 and 108, draw a person who might live or have lived in each home.

Homes and People

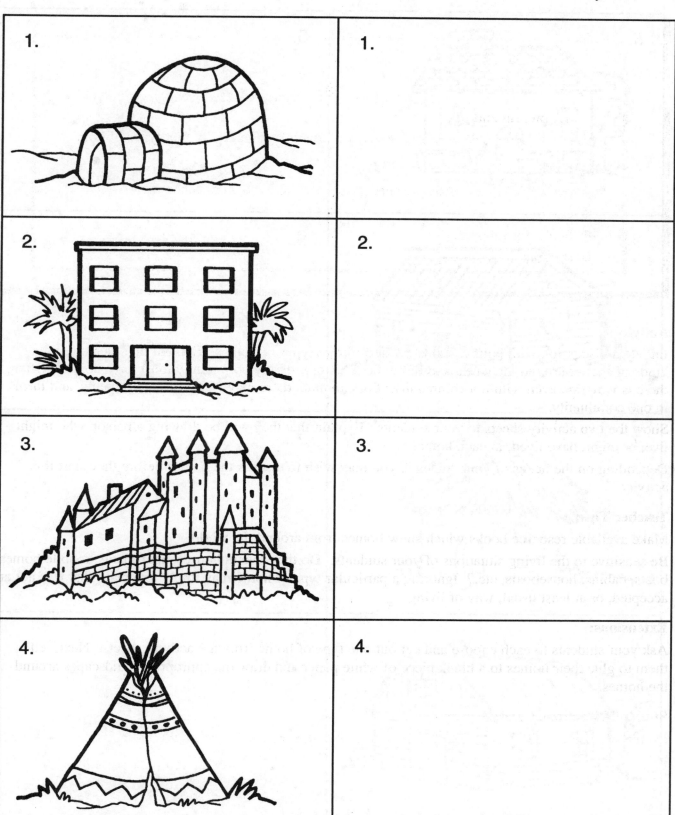

1.	1.
2.	2.
3.	3.
4.	4.

Homes and People (cont.)

5.	5.
6.	6.
7.	7.
8.	8.

Center #4: Activity A

Community Workers

Objectives:

Students will . . .

 . . . recognize jobs within a community.

 . . . identify various community workers.

 . . . classify community workers.

Materials:

❋ single copies of pages 110–112

❋ a copy of page 113 for each student

❋ scissors

Activity:

Have a discussion about workers in your community. Give your students the opportunity to share information about their parents' jobs. Use the Community Workers Headings (page 110) to help the students recognize various categories of workers. Demonstrate how the Community Workers Cards (pages 111 and 112) can be placed under the various headings. Tell your students that they will be using the Headings and Community Workers Cards to organize the jobs into categories. After the jobs have been organized, students will transfer this information to a Community Workers Directory (page 113).

Teacher Tips:

Adjust the amount of time spent on this topic, depending on how much exposure your students have had to community workers and their roles. For best results copy the Community Workers Headings and Cards onto construction paper and laminate them before cutting them out. Then these cards can be taped to the board for demonstration purposes, and they will last longer as a center tool.

Extensions:

Invite community workers to visit your class or take a field trip to a local business.

Student Directions Card:

Use the Community Workers Cards and Headings to classify community workers. Complete a Community Workers Directory.

Community Workers Headings

**Health Care
Services**

**Educational
Services**

**Consumer/Food
Services**

**Protection and
Law Enforcement**

**Maintenance
Services**

Center #4: Activity A

Community Workers Cards

detective	school custodian	grocery store clerk	electrician
ambulance driver	school bus driver	grocery store stock person	plumber
paramedic	911 dispatcher	grocery store manager	construction worker
lab technician	mayor	school cook	telephone crew
pharmacist	city council member	teacher's aide	fast food server

Community Workers Cards *(cont.)*

baker	principal	fire fighter	dentist
florist	librarian	police officer	nurse
road crew	teacher	fire chief	doctor
trash collector	clothing store clerk	police chief	surgeon
street sweeper	waiter/waitress	school superintendent	telephone crew

Center #4: Activity A

Community Workers Directory

Directions: Write the jobs under the proper headings.

Maintenance Services	Consumer/ Food Services	Educational Services	Protection and Law Enforcement	Health Care Services

Center #4: Activity B

Job Applications

Objectives:

Students will . . .

. . . recognize a variety of community jobs.

. . . assess their job skills.

. . . complete job applications.

Materials:

✳ a copy of page 115 for each student

Activity:

With your class, brainstorm a list of community jobs. Post the list in the center for your students to use as a reference. Discuss the process of applying for a job. Have your students each decide on a job (or two) which they would like to have. Encourage your students to focus on their abilities. Tell them that they will be filling out job applications in the center.

Teacher Tips:

Stress the value of all jobs, regardless of training, pay, or prestige. Point out their importance to the maintenance of a successful community.

Demonstrate the process of filling out a job application, highlighting the value of correct spelling and neat writing. Have students complete the application form on page 115.

Extensions:

Obtain real job applications from several community businesses to show your students. Have the personnel director of your school district or of a local business visit the class and discuss his/her job.

Student Directions Card:

Choose a job in which you are interested. Fill out an application for this job.

Application for Employment

Job you are applying for: _____

Full Name: _____ Grade: _____

List four of your favorite pastimes or hobbies.

1. _____ 3. _____
2. _____ 4. _____

List your two favorite subjects.

1. _____
2. _____

List four of your regular chores at home.

1. _____ 3. _____
2. _____ 4. _____

Tell why you would be a good person for this job.

_____

_____

_____

Center #4: Activity B

Application for Employment

Job you are applying for: _____

Full Name: _____ **Grade:** _____

List four of your favorite pastimes or hobbies.

1. _____   3. _____

2. _____   4. _____

List your two favorite subjects.

1. _____

2. _____

List four of your regular chores at home.

1. _____   3. _____

2. _____   4. _____

Tell why you would be a good person for this job.

_____

_____

_____

Center #4: Activity C

Job Search

Objectives:

Students will . . .

. . . read a newspaper for information.

. . . select and analyze job listings.

Materials:

❋ a copy of page 117 for each student

❋ newspaper (job listings)

Activity:

Bring in a local newspaper to share with the students. Discuss the parts of the paper. Focus on the classified section and the job listings. Show your students the format of the job listings and how to extract information from them. Have your students use a newspaper to complete a questionnaire about the job information they discover.

Teacher Tips:

Make a transparency of a job listing to share with your students. Help students identify the important parts of the listing.

You may wish to highlight appropriate job listings in the paper to make it easier for students to locate them.

Extensions:

Have students interview other students as possible employees. Write to the personnel director of a local company and ask what qualifications are required for employment. Invite the manager of a local company to visit your class.

Student Directions Card:

Use a newspaper to complete the Job Search Questionnaire.

Center #4: Activity C

Job Search Questionnaire

Job Title: _____

Job Description: _____

_____

_____

_____

_____

Needed Skills: _____

_____

_____

_____

_____

Salary: _____

Desirability of Job (circle one: 1 is low desirability; 5 is high):

1   2   3   4   5

Center #5: Activity A

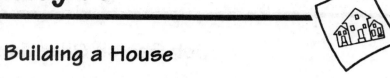

Building a House

> **Objectives:**
>
> *Students will . . .*
>
> . . . follow house construction codes.
>
> . . . build houses.
>
> . . . become part of a community.
>
> **Materials:**
>
> ❄ a house building kit for each student or pair (follow the instructions on page 119)
>
> ❄ housing codes to post (page 120)
>
> ❄ a sample house to share

Activity:

Explain to your students that they will be making a community of model houses. Show students the house building kit they will receive and describe the use of each piece. Demonstrate methods of building a house, using the house building kit (show a sample). Have students build their own houses. After all of the houses have been built, gather them into a community.

Teacher Tips:

Decide on your housing codes before photocopying page 120. Discuss these codes and classroom limitations or rules (e.g., clean-up expectations, available materials) thoroughly before beginning.

If possible, place a large table covered with brown butcher paper in the classroom for students to place their houses on. Allow the students to add trees, parks, roads, etc. Use this opportunity to discuss community decision making.

Extensions:

Ask your students to create buildings for businesses.

Have a town election to select a mayor. Students can campaign and give speeches.

Use a community meeting format to discuss class projects, plans, or problems.

Student Directions Card:

Use a house building kit to build your home. Be sure to follow all of the housing codes.

Center #5: Activity A

Materials for House Building Kits

You will need to prepare bags of materials beforehand for students to use as they build their community. Large, plastic, resealable food storage bags work well for the house building kits. It is best to have one for each student or pair of students. Place the following items in each bag:

- ✂ Two 10 x 12 inch (25.4 x 30.4 cm) pieces of railroad board (house—to include four walls and a roof)

- ✂ One 10 x 3 inch (25.4 x 7.6 cm) piece of brown construction paper (fences, trees)

- ✂ One 10 x 3 inch (25.4 x 7.6 cm) piece of green construction paper (trees, shrubs)

- ✂ Two 4 x 4 inch (10.1 x 10.1 cm) pieces of purple and pink construction paper (flowers, shrubs)

- ✂ One 10 x 1 inch (25.4 x 2.54 cm) strip of clear plastic (windows)

- ✂ One 10 inch (25.4 cm) piece of masking tape (put in the bag or give to students on request)

- ✂ One 10 inch (25.4 cm) piece of cellophane tape (put in the bag or give to students on request)

- ✂ One Paint Pass (index card with the words Paint Pass printed on it; can be used to rent paint and paintbrush for a certain time period)

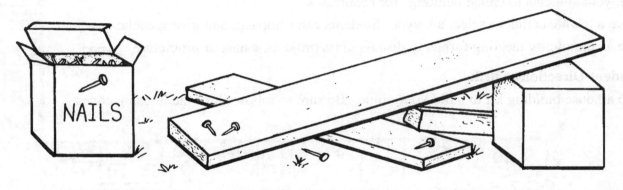

Our Town © 1995 Zephyr Press, Arizona

Center #5: Activity A

Housing Codes

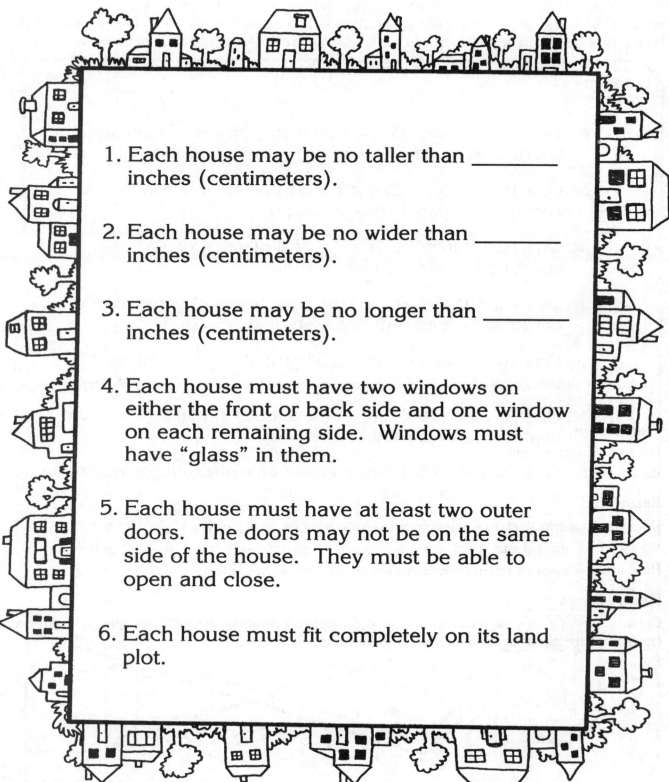

1. Each house may be no taller than _____ inches (centimeters).

2. Each house may be no wider than _____ inches (centimeters).

3. Each house may be no longer than _____ inches (centimeters).

4. Each house must have two windows on either the front or back side and one window on each remaining side. Windows must have "glass" in them.

5. Each house must have at least two outer doors. The doors may not be on the same side of the house. They must be able to open and close.

6. Each house must fit completely on its land plot.

Our Town © 1995 Zephyr Press, Arizona

Center #5: Activity B

Community Service

Objectives:

Students will . . .

　　　. . . participate in a model community service project.

　　　. . . understand the cooperation needed in a community.

　　　. . . plan and create a model community project.

Materials:

❋ a copy of page 122 for each student

❋ various building materials, e.g., clay, paper, tagboard

Activity:

Discuss the importance of all citizens working together to make a community function. Explain to students that they will have an opportunity to contribute to their model community which they created in the last activity. Allow each student to create something to add to the community (e.g., park, bus stop, theater, walking path). Have your students each complete a planning sheet and get teacher and city council approval before beginning. City council approval can be obtained by presenting the idea to the class and having a class vote.

Teacher Tips:

Help your students come up with ideas if they are struggling.

Be sure that a city council approval session can occur each day so that creating will not be held up.

Extensions:

Help your students work in small groups to create additions to the city.

Visit a local park and map it out.

Have a city planner or a parks and recreation employee visit your class.

Student Directions Card:

Create something for your model community. Complete a planning sheet and get approval from your teacher and the city council before you begin creating.

Center #5: Activity B

Community Project Planning Sheet

Name_____

My plan is to create _____

_____

_____

Materials needed: _____

_____

_____

Here is a sketch of my idea.

Teacher approval:_____

Approved by City Council on_____.

Daily Lesson Plan #1

Who Am I?

Objectives:

Students will . . .

    . . . understand the importance of community workers.

    . . . recognize the roles of community workers.

    . . . identify community workers by job descriptions.

Materials:

❖ single copies of pages 124 and 125

Activities:

Discuss the topic of community workers and their roles. Use the Who Am I? cards to play a community workers game. The descriptions can be read by the teacher or a student while the other students guess the workers' identities. Begin by reading only the first clue. If the students cannot identify the worker, read the second clue. If the identity is still not guessed, read all of the clues.

Teacher Tips:

To prepare the Who Am I? Cards, copy them onto construction paper and laminate before cutting them out.

Adjust the amount of time spent on this topic, depending on the amount of exposure your students have had to community workers and their roles.

Extensions:

Ask parents or relatives to come in for a visit and share information about their jobs. Be sure to include at-home workers.

Have the students act out community jobs while other students guess who they are.

Challenge your students to create their own Who Am I? Cards to use.

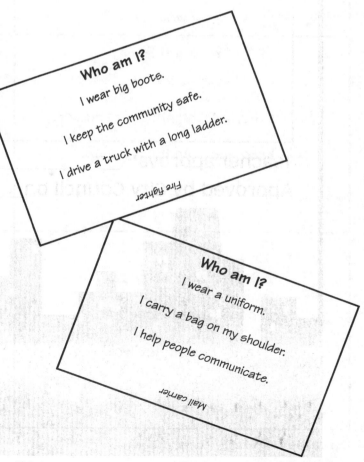

Who am I?

I wear big boots.

I keep the community safe.

I drive a truck with a long ladder.

Fire fighter

Who am I?

I wear a uniform.

I carry a bag on my shoulder.

I help people communicate.

Mail carrier

Daily Lesson Plan #1

Who Am I? Cards

Who am I? I wear big boots. I keep the community safe. I drive a truck with a long ladder. *Fire fighter*	**Who am I?** I wear a uniform. I carry a bag on my shoulder. I help people communicate. *Mail carrier*
Who am I? I wear business clothes. I work in city hall. I help the city run smoothly. *Mayor*	**Who am I?** I wear a white coat. I use a chair that moves up and down. I take care of people's teeth. *Dentist*
Who am I? I wear a badge. I drive a car with lights on the top. I keep the community safe. *Police officer*	**Who am I?** I wear heavy gloves. I drive a big truck. I keep the community clean. *Trash collector*
Who am I? I wear a white coat. I carry a stethoscope. I help people get well. *Doctor*	**Who am I?** I wear regular clothes. I write on a chalkboard. I help students learn. *Teacher*

Daily Lesson Plan #1

Who Am I? Cards (cont.)

Who am I? I do not wear a uniform. I help people find information. I handle books. *Librarian*	**Who am I?** I do not always wear a uniform. I drive a large vehicle. I take children to and from school. *Schoolbus driver*
Who am I? I wear a tall white hat. I use many pots and pans. I prepare food. *Cook*	**Who am I?** I work outdoors. I wear an orange vest. I help keep the roads in good condition. *Road worker*
Who am I? I wear an apron. I use a cash register. I sell food to the community. *Grocery store clerk*	**Who am I?** I usually wear regular clothes. I use rulers and pencils. I design buildings. *Architect*
Who am I? I wear a uniform. I have a gas pump and tools. I help keep cars running. *Gas station attendant*	**Who am I?** I wear a white coat. I give shots. I keep your pets healthy. *Veterinarian*

Our Town © 1995 Zephyr Press, Arizona

#2033 Thematic Learning Centers

Daily Lesson Plan #2

Community Name

> **Objectives:**
>
> *Students will . . .*
>
>   . . . practice using a democratic procedure.
>
>   . . . decide on a name for their model community.
>
> **Materials:**
>
> ❖ examples of community names

Activities:

Lead a discussion about democratic procedures (e.g., majority rules, everyone is allowed a vote). Begin selecting a name for the model community (created in Center #5: Activities A and B) by sharing some examples of possible names. Include names from your local area and others of particular interest. Allow your students to brainstorm ideas and record all of them. Once brainstorming has been completed, review the list. Allow the students to discuss and vote on their favorite two or three names until the list is reduced to four names. In the final vote, the students should each vote only once for their favorite community names. Once a name has been selected, celebrate!

Older students may benefit from discussing and debating the names before voting. Younger students may, however, regard any discussion of their suggestions as a personal criticism. In this case, voting without discussion may be better.

Teacher Tips:

When brainstorming community names, be sure that the students know that all suggestions are valid and appreciated whether or not they are selected as the final name.

Be sure to discuss the importance of being a good sport, since your community will have only one name.

Extensions:

Have your students create a banner with your community name on it.

Challenge your students to each write a paragraph describing your model community.

Students may want to make a town sign welcoming people to your community.

Daily Lesson Plan #3

Trust Walk

Objectives:

Students will . . .

    . . . participate in a cooperative relationship.

    . . . be responsible for each other.

    . . . be responsive to each other.

Materials:
- ❖ blindfolds for half of the class
- ❖ outdoor area with few obstacles

Activities:

Discuss the importance of cooperation in community environments, such as schools, families, neighborhoods, businesses. Introduce the concepts of dependability and trust and point out their connection to cooperation. Tell the students they are going to participate in a cooperative relationship where they will need to be dependable and trusting. Explain the trust walk to the students:

1. Students will each have a partner for the entire activity.
2. Partners will take turns leading and being led.
3. The students being led will wear blindfolds to hide their eyes while their partners guide them on a walk.
4. The people doing the guiding must warn and inform their partners about all of the obstacles in the way, for example, curbs, steps, and changes in surfaces.
5. The guiding students will also stop and allow the blindfolded partners to discover interesting textures and items, such as grass, poles, rocks, leaves, and walls.
6. After a specified time, partners will change roles.

Teacher Tips:

Be sure to demonstrate the trust walk responsibilities by guiding a blindfolded student. Point out the importance of viewing the world from the perspective of the blindfolded person. Students need to be aware of things near the feet, head, and ears of blindfolded partners. Demonstrate the appropriate way to link arms to ensure a safe walk.

Be sure to pair students carefully. Avoid combinations that you suspect will not lead to a positive experience.

Extensions:

Have students write about their experiences. Ask them each to draw an object that they discovered when they were blindfolded.

Bloom's Taxonomy

Analysis

Write five rules that would apply to community life.

ANALYSIS

Teacher's Directions: Copy this page onto construction paper or card stock. Cut out and laminate the shape. This activity can be posted in a center for student use or used as seat work by individual students.

Bloom's Taxonomy

Synthesis

Compose a song or write an advertisement which describes your community.

SYNTHESIS

Teacher's Directions: Copy this page onto construction paper or card stock. Cut out and laminate the shape. This activity can be posted in a center for student use or used as seat work by individual students.

Bloom's Taxonomy

Evaluation

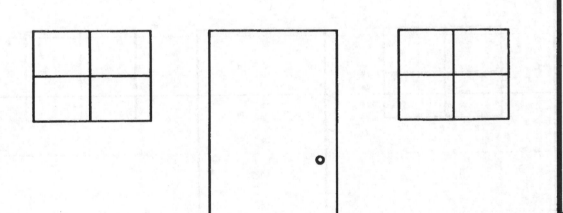

Create a survey to evaluate community members' attitudes about your community.

EVALUATION

Teacher's Directions: Copy this page onto construction paper or card stock. Cut out and laminate the shape. This activity can be posted in a center for student use or used as seat work by individual students.

Problem Solving

Activity #1

Read the situation below and write down your ideas.

> Your community is considering building a movie theater. It would be a welcome addition to the community, but it would create more traffic on an already crowded road. What are some possible solutions?

Write your ideas here:

_____

_____

_____

_____

_____

_____

_____

_____

Problem Solving

Activity #2

Read the situation below and write down your ideas.

Because cigarette smoke can be harmful, your community wants to become smoke free. Smokers in the community are against this. Is it a good idea to enforce a smoke-free community? Why or why not?

Write your ideas here:

_____

_____

_____

_____

_____

_____

_____

_____

_____

Problem Solving

Activity #3

Read the situation below and write down your ideas.

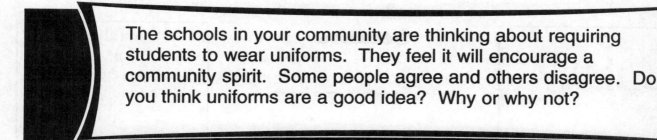

The schools in your community are thinking about requiring students to wear uniforms. They feel it will encourage a community spirit. Some people agree and others disagree. Do you think uniforms are a good idea? Why or why not?

Write your ideas here:

_____

_____

_____

_____

_____

_____

_____

_____

_____

Connections Activity Sheet

Communities

How Are They Connected?

because

_____

_____

_____

_____

because   **because**

_____   _____

_____   _____

_____   _____

_____   _____

Teacher's Directions: Use this page as a culminating activity. Assess your students' understanding of the information taught in the "Communities" unit, explore and debate issues, or increase flexible thinking in relation to the communities topic. You may wish to make related vocabulary words available for your students to use. This page is designed to encourage your students to explore and expand their concepts of making connections.

Student Directions Cards

Center #1

My Unique Family

Using the materials provided, create each member of your family. On the back of the portraits write things about each person which make him or her unique.

Center #2

Me Book

Using the pages provided, create a Me Book. Use color and detail in your work. Be sure to write and spell carefully.

Center #3

Me Puzzle

Use the drawing paper to draw a picture of yourself, including as much detail as possible. Then glue your drawing to a piece of construction paper. Next, draw light cutting lines on the back of the construction paper. Make eight sections about the same size but different shapes. Now, cut on the lines to create your puzzle. Store your puzzle in a large envelope.

Student Directions Cards *(cont.)*

Center #4
This Is Me

Trace the person pattern onto a large piece of paper. Write your name on the back of your traced person. Find pictures in magazines which show things about yourself—likes, hobbies, personality traits, favorite colors, food, movies, etc. Cut out the magazine pictures and glue them onto your paper, creating a collage.

Center #5
My Family Tree

Draw a tree on a large piece of paper. Use finger paints to create leaves on your tree. Make one leaf for each member of your family. When the paint is dry, use a marker to label each leaf with a family member's name. Be sure to include yourself.

Center #1: Activity A
Endangered Species

Put together the Endangered Species Puzzle. Use the facts on the puzzle and any other resources to complete the Endangered Species Activity Sheet.

Student Directions Cards *(cont.)*

Center #1: Activity B
Masks

Choose an animal outline to make into a mask.
Color your mask as realistically as you can.

Center #2: Activity A
My Environment

Pretend that you are looking through a window at a man-made environment in which you spend some of your time each day. Draw this environment within the window outline.

Center #2: Activity B
Shaping the Environment

Using a paper plate as your base, create an environment out of clay. Include at least five different landforms in your environment.

Center #3: Activity A
People and the Environment

Create a poster encouraging three behaviors which have a positive effect on the environment. Be sure to follow the criteria.

Center #3: Activity B
Pitch In!

Using a large paper bag, create a usable trash bag with an environmental message.

Center #4: Activity A
Growing Beans

Plant a bean. Record its daily growth on an index card. Be sure to water your bean plant.

Center #4: Activity B

Plants, Plants, Plants!

Using the Plant Parts Activity Sheet, create a unique flowering plant. Glue your plant to a plain sheet of paper. Label all of the parts.

Center #5: Activity A

Pollution in Our Environment

Make a trash fact pack! Fill in the missing information on each trash can and then cut the cans out. Punch a hole in the tops of the cans and attach them together with a paper fastener.

Center #5: Activity B

Home Sweet Home!

Color and cut the nature Cover-Up Activity Sheets. Assemble this project by gluing the first sheet over the second. Do not glue the windows shut!

Student Directions Cards (cont.)

Center #1: Activity A
Passport

Using a passport definition puzzle or a dictionary, complete a passport.

Center #1: Activity B
My Community

Create a map of your community on a piece of large, white paper. Include local businesses, schools, libraries, parks, etc.

Center #1: Activity C
Community Workers

Draw a community worker on each side of your activity sheet. Describe each worker's job in two to four sentences.

Student Directions Cards (cont.)

Center #2: Activity A
Money Maker

Use the money outlines to design your own money. Create at least three different denominations.

Center #2: Activity B
Bank It!

Draw cards from the expense box. Use the bank account sheet to record your expenses.

Center #2: Activity C
Logo Maker

Design a simple logo for your community. Be sure to follow the posted criteria.

Student Directions Cards *(cont.)*

Center #3: Activity A
Community Newspaper

Make a rough draft of your newspaper page. After showing it to your teacher, make a final draft in black pen.

Center #3: Activity B
Regional Foods

Write a recipe on the activity sheet. Use one food which is from your community or state.

Center #3: Activity C
Types of Homes

On the right sides of activity pages 107 and 108, draw a person who might live or have lived in each home.

Student Directions Cards (cont.)

Center #4: Activity A
Community Workers

Use the Community Workers Cards and Headings to classify community workers. Complete a Community Workers Directory.

Center #4: Activity B
Job Applications

Choose a job in which you are interested. Fill out an application for this job.

Center #4: Activity C
Job Search

Use a newspaper to complete the Job Search Questionnaire.

Center #5: Activity A
Building a House

Use a house building kit to build your home. Be sure to follow all of the housing codes.

Center #5: Activity B
Community Service

Create something for your model community. Complete a planning sheet and get approval from your teacher and the city council before you begin creating.